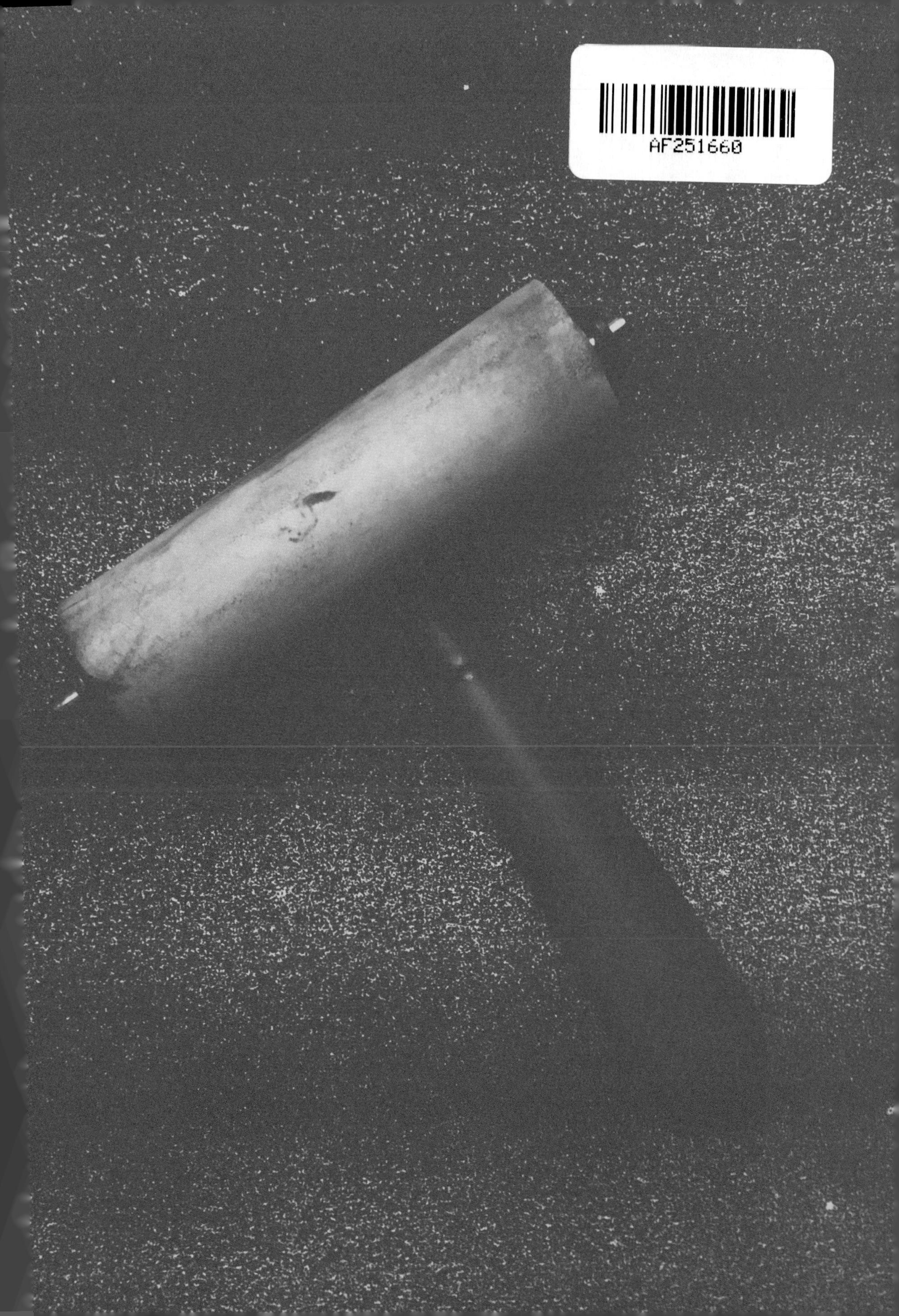

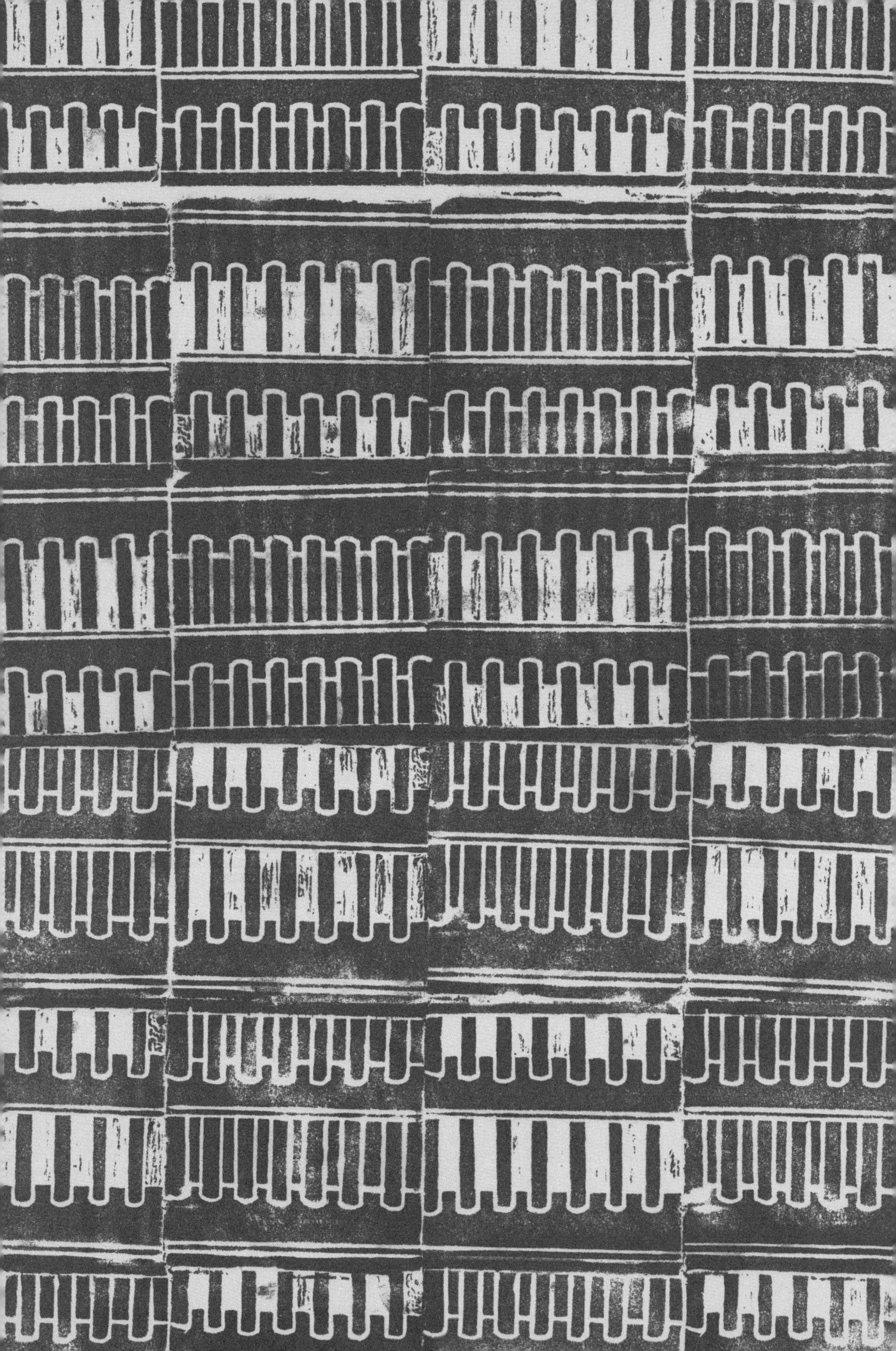

Salvador Herrera, *Pattern*, 2018

CARVING OUT RIGHTS

FROM INSIDE THE PRISON INDUSTRIAL COMPLEX

EDITED BY
AARON HUGHES, SARAH ROSS, AND TARA BETTS

HAT & BEARD PRESS | LOS ANGELES

Copyright © 2021 by Hat & Beard Press, Los Angeles.
Edited by Aaron Hughes, Sarah Ross, and Tara Betts.

Essays and interviews compiled and edited by Aaron Hughes and Sarah Ross.
Poetry compiled and edited by Tara Betts.

"Poem for July 4, 1994" from *Shake Loose My Skin: New and Selected Poems*
by Sonia Sanchez reprinted with permission of Beacon Press, Boston.
Copyright © 1999 by Sonia Sanchez.
All other poems printed with permission of poets.

Foam block prints in this book are from Prison + Neighborhood Arts/Education Project
classes at Stateville Prison taught by Aaron Hughes and William Estrada.
Artwork edited by Giselle Mira-Diaz and printed with permission of the artists.
Photos by Alice Kim and Sarah-Ji Rhee printed with permission of photographers.

This book was designed, typeset, and made into pages by Aaron Hughes.
The text was set in typefaces Georgia and TradeGothic LT CondEighteen.
Cover design by Damon Locks.
Printed by Oddi Sales in Bosnia and Herzegovina.

ISBN 978-1-7327345-6-2

This book was produced in partnership with Invisible Republic, an arts nonprofit,
and programming initiative of Future Roots, Inc., a 501c3 organization.

hatandbeard.com | invisiblerepublic.org

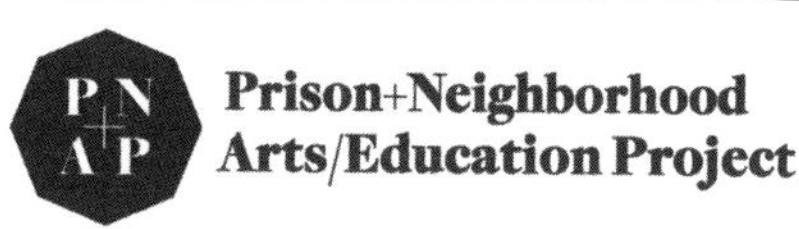

Contents

Thanks & Acknowledgments

A big thank you to the faculty, staff, and members of the Prison + Neighborhood Arts/Education Project (P+NAP) who work with artists, writers, and scholars at Stateville Prison with a vision of liberation and abolition. Thank you to all the artists and students at Stateville Prison who demonstrate every day the radical idea of exercising human rights against the grain. Their work and spirit shape the demands for justice we all need to hear.

Thank you to Meredith Stern for sharing her *Universal Declaration of Human Rights Print Project* and providing inspiration for the prints in this book. We also want to thank our comrades in the P+NAP Art Team (Damon Locks and Anna Martine Whitehead) for their support and guidance throughout this process.

William Estrada generously shared artwork from his 2018 P+NAP class for this book. Alice Kim, Sarah-Ji Rhee, Elizabeth Sisco, Joseph Dole, and Tamms Year Ten also shared their photographs and graphics. Giselle Mira-Diaz meticulously edited the prints. Fred Sasaki supported us with poetry layout. Holly Amos compiled contributor biographies. Kevin Basl helped with text editing. And Jerome Grand and Josh MacPhee supported us with page layout. We couldn't have made this book without all of you. Thank you!

The editors would like to thank their friends and family for patience and support throughout the process of making this book. There is always less visible labor that makes any creative or intellectual pursuit possible. We couldn't do this without them.

A special thanks to all the people who generously support P+NAP's work, especially the Illinois Humanities, Field Foundation, and Invisible Republic whose generous financial support helped make this book possible.

Meredith Stern

FOREWORD

I embarked upon the project of creating a series of prints on the Universal Declaration of Human Rights in 2016. It was before the presidential election and nomination of Donald Trump as the Republican candidate. It was also a year marked by massive community organizing, notably the Standing Rock and Dakota Access Pipeline Protests and Black Lives Matter demonstrations about the deaths of Black people by police, including Philando Castile, Deborah Danner, Alton Sterling, Joseph Mann, Abdirahman Abdi, Paul O'Neal, Korryn Gaines, Sylville Smith, Terence Crutcher, Keith Lamont Scott, Alfred Olango, and Bruce Kelley Jr.

It was clear to me that no matter who became president, human rights violations were endemic around the country, and violence and injustice was continuing to disproportionately target people who are Black, Native, immigrants, and everyone in our society deemed "nonwhite." It was also clear that mass mobilization, protest, and grassroots organizing was crucial to combatting institutional, systemic, and individual racism—and the white supremacy that is rampant and embedded in every aspect of our society.

Human rights violations are most blatantly evident in the policing, imprisonment, and detention of people in the United States. There is growing awareness of the "school to prison pipeline," the devastation of the racist "war on drugs," and the mass incarceration of Black men. However, we are far away from preventing these harmful policies from continuing to do harm, and from making any sort of reparations to communities that have been affected by these policies, or dismantling the white supremacy that continues to prop up our entire system.

When I first started working with grassroots organizations, a popular slogan was "educate, agitate, organize." Loretta Ross introduced me to the Universal Declaration of Human Rights through a talk she gave in Providence, Rhode Island. It is a useful framework for understanding systemic injustice in our society but there is currently no legal requirement for the United States to comply with the document. While it is by no means perfect, it can be an entry point for understanding human rights on many levels in our country. I believe this document can be one potential educational tool for grassroots organizing on human rights.

One of the most brilliant writers of our time, Toni Morrison, recently passed. She wrote a series of children's books, including one she wrote with Slade Morrison, called *The Big Box*. It poetically introduces kids to the concept of imprisonment and systemic injustice. There's a line that's been circling in my head since she passed: "If freedom is handled just your way then it's not my freedom or free."

Jelani Cobb's idea of "contingency citizenship" and Alicia Garza's description of the tenuous citizenship for Black folks eloquently express the heart of racial injustice in this country. To work for human rights justice we must recognize that people are not protected equally, and this is most evident within the criminal "justice" system. We must dismantle the policing and prison system and continue to build a massive resistance against white supremacy in every aspect of our society.

In order for a more just world to emerge through our collective resistance, it is crucial that the voices of those most negatively affected by these issues be at the center of human rights work. This art project centers the voices of folks at the Stateville Prison in Illinois who created images inspired by the Universal Declaration of Human Rights through an artistic partnership with the Prison + Neighborhood Arts/Education Project. The articles they chose to illustrate reflect the pressing issues within our policing system, such as cruel and inhumane punishment, unjust incarceration of innocent people, and the inhumane treatment of people as slaves within the prison system. The art created is visually beautiful and inspiring and demonstrates the cultural leadership they bring to this movement.

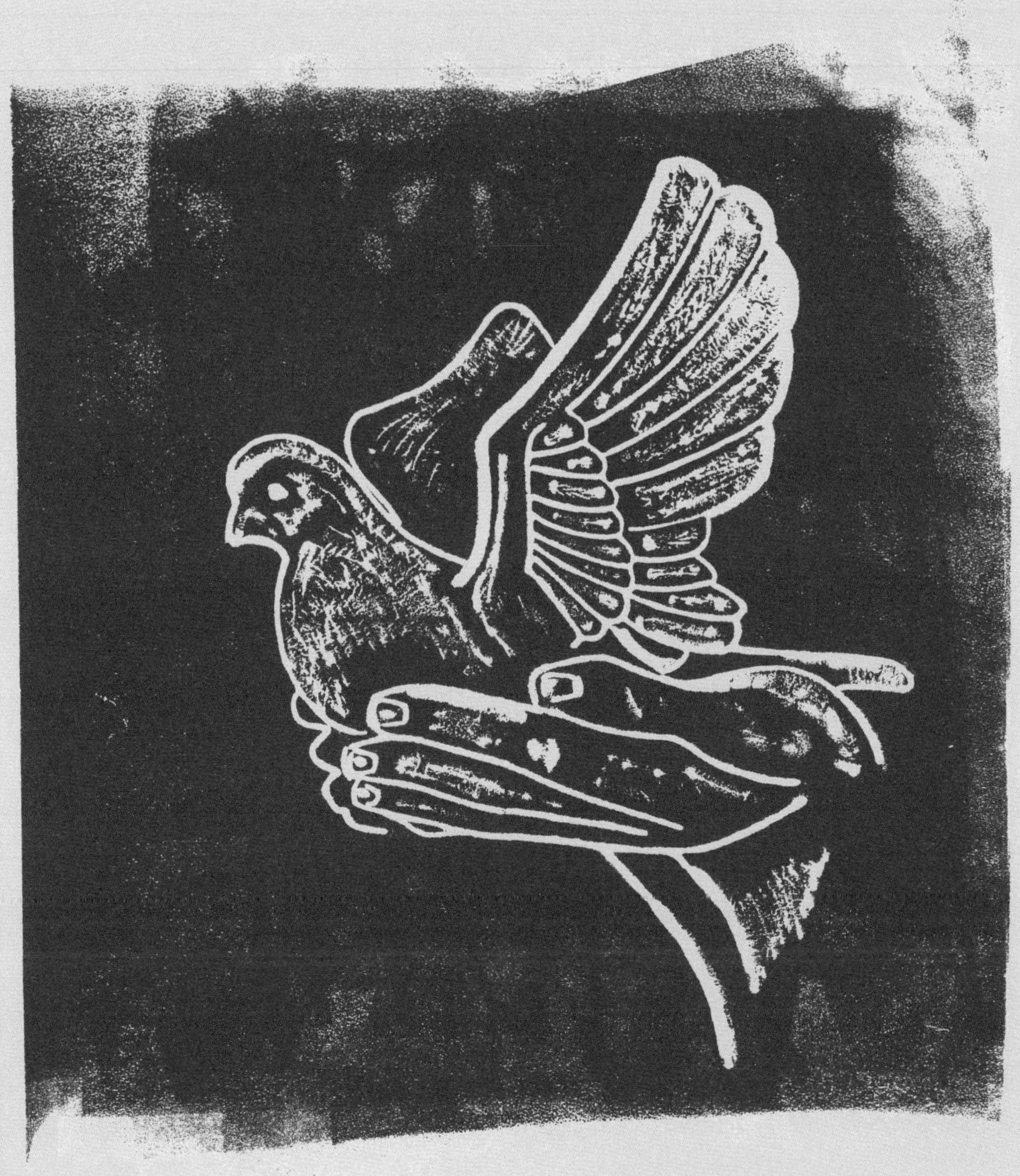

Charles McLaurin, *The Peaceful Symbolism*, 2018

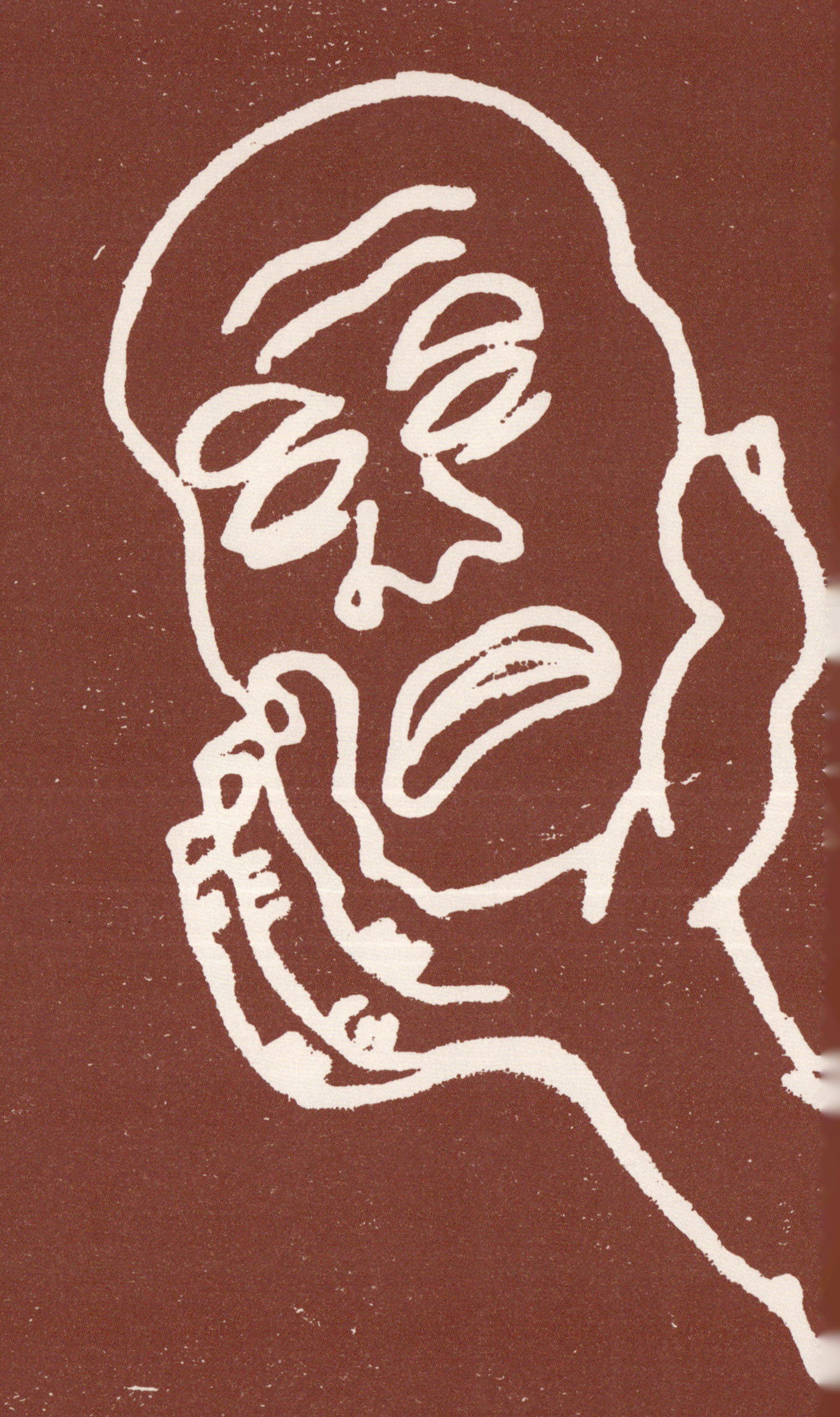

Aaron Hughes

INTRODUCTION: BUILDING A CULTURE OF HUMAN RIGHTS FROM BELOW

« Aryules Bivens, *Article 6* (Detail), 2018

*Our common goal is to obtain the human rights that America has
been denying us. We can never get civil rights in America until our
human rights are first restored. We will never be recognized as
citizens there until we are first recognized as humans.*[1]
　　　—Malcolm X, "Racism: The Cancer that Is Destroying America"
　　　　　　　　　　　　　　　Egyptian Gazette (Aug. 25 1964)

What does it mean to "carve out" rights from inside the prison industrial
complex?

It means the people on the inside are the ones articulating what rights
are and are not. It means the people most impacted by institutional oppression and state violence have an opportunity to learn from, respond to, and
strategically use the Universal Declaration of Human Rights (UDHR)
as a tool to seek justice and liberation. It means acknowledging the inherent
contradictions of the UDHR and its crafting by nation states, including the
United States, actively invested in undermining human rights through settler
colonialism, imperialism, and racial capitalism. It means seeking liberation, restorative justice, and what Angela Davis calls "abolition democracy."
It means building a culture of human rights from below.

—

Standing in a corner of the small classroom at Stateville Prison, a maximum-
security prison in Crest Hill, Illinois, Aryules Bivens uses the top of
a bookshelf as a drawing table. He slowly sketches out a figure holding
in their hand a mask of their removed frowning face. Checking in with him,
he tells me over and over again that he is new to drawing and wants to
get better. I let him know he is doing great. His lines are clean and have
a consistent unwavering quality that quickly bring form to concept.

The emerging faceless figure is somewhat haunting to me. Aryules reveals the power of his design as he shares the article from the UDHR it references. Article Six reads, "Everyone has the right to recognition everywhere as a person before the law." Yet, before the law, Aryules' figure is faceless—presumably personless.

This simple design highlights the contradictions of the status quo concepts of safety, security, and justice in the United States. Every day, people incarcerated in the U.S. assert their status as human beings, and demand to be recognized as a "person before the law." Yet, under the guise of justice, they are denied this human right and instead suffer the indignities of a discriminatory judicial system, psychological, physical, and sexual violence, not to mention the terrible living conditions inside the carceral system.

As Aryules transfers his design to a Styrofoam block and begins to slowly carve out each line, I think more and more about these contradictions and how his figure haunts not just me, but the ideals of rights and justice in the United States. Aryules and his fellow students in my printmaking class called "Make Your Mark & Fly Your Flag" know and see clearly the normalized contradictions that many people in the United States are blind to. They live with these contradictions as they negotiate an institution inherently blind to their humanity. Despite this, the students see one another not as faceless numbers in a vast dehumanizing institution, but as creative dignified people, inspiring artists to learn from, and friends to grow with.

In the classroom, away from the constant surveillance of the prison, the students have created a kind of sanctuary in the midst of an otherwise hot, stark, and stressful place. They have transformed the classroom into a space for reclaiming their voices, rights, and humanity—a space of resistance. Creating this space of learning, trust, and vulnerable critical engagement is central to the work of the Prison + Neighborhood Arts/Education Project (P+NAP), the college level arts and humanities program I work with. Informed by a Black feminist abolitionist framework, P+NAP focuses on fostering the exchange of knowledge between people inside prison and people in different Chicago neighborhoods.

The project carries on the legacy of the late Dr. Margaret Burroughs, a profoundly influential Chicago Black artist who helped launch the South Side Community Art Center and co-founded the DuSable Museum of African American History. As a volunteer she taught art and creative writing at Stateville Prison until 2010, the year she passed away at the age of 95. Six years later, during my first art class at Stateville, a number of the students

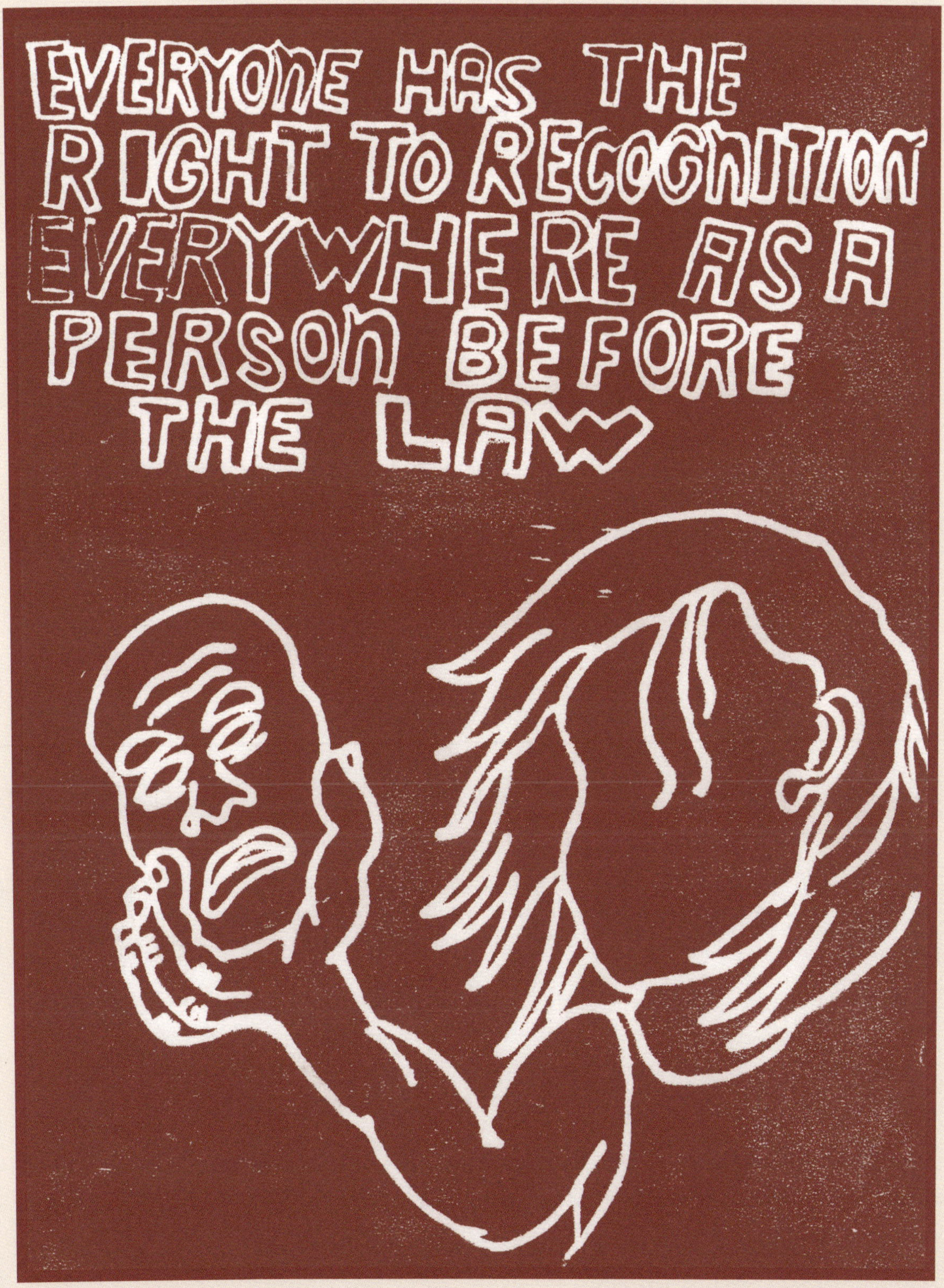

Aryules Bivens, *UDHR Article 6*, 2018

remembered her fondly. One of them shared a pamphlet Dr. Burroughs made on different art techniques. She taught at Stateville for over 25 years, inspiring students to transform their cells into studios.

As a white male Iraq War veteran, following in this legacy is a challenge and a process of endless learning, failing, and growing. Simultaneously, walking through the prison feels eerily familiar. Stateville Prison's 33-foot high concrete walls adorned with 10 weaponized towers remind me keenly of the perimeter walls surrounding countless military installations I frequented during my time in the National Guard. Prisons and military installations share a veneer of authority-in-decay. From the cracks in the old massive concrete walls, to the sparkling waxed concrete floor complemented by chipped paint and leaking pipes, to the halfhearted performance of power through bureaucratic functions, both prisons and military installations simultaneously provoke in me a sense of awe, bewilderment, alienation, and familiarity.

More broadly, the military and prison industrial complexes share a relationship to American exceptionalism—the notion that the United States is unique: always the best, right, and just. It is through this frame of American exceptionalism that the United States justifies war, occupation, torture, extra-legal detention, mass incarceration, and the gross human rights violations that people locked up in the carceral system across the U.S. face on a daily basis. Furthermore, the U.S. weaponizes human rights to justify military interventions in sovereign nations. For example, despite attacks on women's rights in the U.S., one might recall the concerns voiced about women's rights in Afghanistan as a justification for the continued occupation there. This frame of American exceptionalism is the same framework that suggests our justice system is actually just, despite ample evidence to the contrary.

I raise this issue of American exceptionalism and the connections between the prison and military industrial complexes not because of my personal relationship to each, but to point out the importance of building a culture of human rights from below. As important and visionary as the UDHR is, the human rights violations committed by the United States and other founding nation states undermine the declaration, and human rights in general. Human rights are reclaimed, gain legitimacy, and a sense of their truly transformative and liberatory power when they are defined from the grassroots, by people most impacted by institutional racism and state violence. The artworks featured in this book bring these crucial perspectives to the UDHR. Like Aryules' simple depiction capturing a complicated issue, incarcerated people have a great deal of insight into what human rights need to look like if they are going to truly be universal and inalienable.

—

Looking around the room, Aryules is the only student standing. The rest are sitting around two wobbly tables pushed together. To my left are two long-time P+NAP artists, Darrell W. Fair and Charles McLaurin. They are both brilliant artists with their own artistic styles. They are continuously encouraging and mentoring the whole class, including me. Next to them is Juan Luna, an extremely engaged student who is always ready to share a social justice perspective. He is also working on his college diploma through a P+NAP partnership with the University Without Walls program out of Northeastern Illinois University. Past him, towards the far end of the table, is Alan "Wolf" Christensen, a lover of rock and roll, and a serious and determined student committed to getting his work just right. Next is Marshall W. Stewart, a skilled artist and another scholar in the P+NAP University Without Walls program. At the back of the room is Carlos J. Ayala, a talented artist with a willingness to experiment. He is continuously going beyond class expectations making artworks that demonstrate his expertise. Next to him is Salvador Herrera, a quiet diligent illustrator, and Rickey L. Quezada, a reflective intellectual ready to push the conversation. Sitting to their side is Alex Koehler, a quiet individual with a knack for drawing. Then Jeff Campbell, a serious student with a clear commitment to getting things done right, and Willie M. McGee, a cheerful and joyful guy excited to learn and share.

This is a constellation of people that would not otherwise come together. Yet here we are collectively working on being artists, seeking answers to profound questions, creating knowledge, and beginning to enact a culture of human rights. Their commitment to the work is clear, and it is not lost on me that each pen stroke outside of class is a negotiation. Two people are assigned to each small Stateville cell, providing only enough room for one person at a time to sit at the metal desk.

As they work on their designs, industrial fans hum and noise from other classes reverberates off the walls. The students, who are mostly older than I am at 38, speak softly and listen intently to each other's voices barely audible over the cacophony. They are discussing what it means to carve out rights from within the prison industrial complex. They hold all the contradictions while discussing the history of rights, questioning the institutions that uphold and deny rights, and imagining what rights should be and how to demand them.

As we listen to each other carefully, novel ideas emerge for understanding rights, imagining freedom, and enacting democracy.

Angela Davis makes this need to radically reimagine a democracy founded in abolition clear in her book *Abolition Democracy: Beyond Empire, Prisons, and Torture*. She writes:

> *Du Bois pointed out that in order to fully abolish the oppressive conditions produced by slavery, new democratic institutions would have to be created. Because this did not occur, black people encountered new forms of slavery—from debt peonage and the convict lease system to segregated and second-class education. The prison system continues to carry out this terrible legacy. It has become a receptacle for all of those human beings who bear the inheritance of the failure to create abolition democracy in the aftermath of slavery. And this inheritance is not only born by black prisoners, but by poor Latino, Native American, Asians, and white prisoners. Moreover, its use as such a receptacle for people who are deemed the detritus of society is on the rise throughout the world.[2]*
>
> —

Helping the class research ideas for their art projects, I share Meredith Stern's *Universal Declaration of Human Rights Print Project* booklet in which she carved a block for each Article of the UDHR. The simplicity and beauty of Stern's powerful prints along with the global scope of the UDHR inspire the class to follow in Stern's footsteps and create a set of prints for each of the 30 articles of the UDHR. This inspiration and the creative work that emerges follows in a tradition of everyday people and grassroots movements utilizing the frame of human rights in their struggles for justice and liberation. This tradition can be seen in the 1970 call for dignity by the United Prisoners Union in California. The *Goals of the Prisoner's Union* document states:

> *For centuries persons charged and convicted of crimes have been looked upon and treated as less than human beings [...] the prisoner, the convict and the ex-convict are treated with extreme hostility and oppression more because of their being poor or members of racial minorities and having reduced life circumstances of ill fortune, than their being persons who have reduced worth or who are less deserving of dignity.[3]*

Multiple essays in *Carving Out Rights* highlight connections between human rights and grassroots movements. Christophe Ringer's essay, "The Future of Human Rights," touches on the Civil Rights Congress' 1951 petition to the United Nations titled, "We Charge Genocide: The Crime of Government Against the Negro People." He connects the work of the Civil Rights Congress to the Chicago Torture Justice Memorials' fight for reparation for police torture, and the youth-led organization We Charge Genocide's report to the United Nations, "Police Violence Against Chicago's Youth of Color." In the essay "Are Rights Truly Self Evident?" Benny Rios Donjuan lifts up the Civil Rights Movement's fight against segregation and the United Farm Workers' organizing campaigns to secure better wages and worker rights. Barbara Ransby's essay, "Reflections on Teaching at Stateville Prison," connects the many calls for abolition and restorative justice by the Movement for Black Lives and Black Lives Matter with the limitations of the United States legal system and the need for truly universal inalienable human rights from below.

—

In the class we prepare for the print production by carefully reviewing each article of the UDHR and discussing the points that stand out. Then each artist chooses two articles that speak to them and develops correlating designs. They trace each design onto foam blocks, in reverse. Security concerns at the prison do not permit us to utilize traditional block carving tools. The foam blocks, carved with pens and pencils, are the closest proxy. To print, the students roll ink out on cardboard scraps and then carefully ink the blocks before meticulously aligning and placing a sheet of paper. We use our hands, or the bottom of ink jars, to burnish and hand-press the prints. While some details in the prints get lost, the meaningful content and personal designs overshadow any limitations of our alternative, rudimentary techniques.

For example, Salvador Herrera's design for Article 9 ("No one shall be subjected to arbitrary arrest, detention, or exile") features the Statue of Liberty with her torch-bearing hand outstretched, intersecting with the word "freedom" scrawled across the top of the print. Freedom and liberty, these are rights he is currently denied. Alan "Wolf" Christensen carves a print for Article 10 which references rights to a fair trial. In the print the figure in the foreground wears a shirt with the abbreviations "DOC" (Department of Corrections), standing before a judge. What kind of fair trial is offered to those already deemed criminals?

Darrell W. Fair's print covers Article 11 ("Everyone charged with a penal offense has the right to be presumed innocent until proved guilty according to law in a public trial at which he has had all the guarantees necessary for his defense"). In the design, police force a figure to the ground as they scream out, alluding to Darrell's own experience with unexpectedly being detained and tortured into a false confession by the police. Juan Luna's design for Article 14 ("Everyone has the right to seek and to enjoy in other countries asylum from persecution") features a figure in the foreground holding a voided U.S. visa, a reference to the many asylum seekers and refugees denied status, safety, and security in the United States.

Each step of the printmaking process provides time and space for students to reflect on the ways the UDHR is simultaneously aspirational, strategic, and fraught with the legacy of the violence of its founding states. Questions emerge: If these are human rights, why are we not afforded them? Are the State of Illinois and the United States of America not directly violating our human rights? Are we not human?

It is clear to the artists that, at home and abroad, the 30 separate articles of the UDHR articulating inalienable universal rights are still ideals, not norms. This has been made painfully clear during the COVID-19 pandemic. The pandemic exposes the extent of overcrowding, unsafe living conditions, and lack of adequate health care throughout the carceral system in the United States. Specifically, due to the inability to physically distance, access to consistent good health care, and scarcity of sanitation and cleaning supplies, COVID-19 has spread rapidly, with the worst example being San Quentin State Prison in California. As of August 2020, 25 people have died there and more than 2,600 people have tested positive.[4] Overall, people incarcerated are five times more likely to be infected with COVID-19 than the national average[5] and the death rate is also higher at an average of 39 deaths for every 100,000 people incarcerated.[6] Illinois' prisons are no exception, with their serious lack of sanitation and cleaning supplies posted daily on the Department of Corrections' website. P+NAP worked with a coalition of educators and artists to buy and deliver soap to people incarcerated.

—

As we carve the foam blocks we also carve out a space for an emerging culture of human rights rooted in the theories of participation, abolition, and democracy. Collectively, in our small classroom, for three hours a week, we shape a different relationship with each other that rejects the norms of the prison industrial complex and embraces a revolutionary humanities discourse committed to listening, learning, and building freedom.

As we hand-print editions of each foam block, the room quickly fills with our conversation and our drying prints. We place prints of each Article all around the room, on the tables, chairs, and across the floor. The prints overflow into the common area between the classrooms. A bit of commotion stirs as we move around the room and the common area looking for a free spot to place the next print hot off the press. We are working together as peers to create prints that demand human rights. A number of us recognize the power in Carlos J. Ayala's print for Article 4 with the words "let freedom ring" centered above a dove breaking through chains. The Article begins, "No one shall be held in slavery or servitude." Ideas of freedom echo throughout the school as other students pass by, stop, look and read the prints, taking time to admire the craft and message.

The prints and the commotion temporarily rupture the dismal bureaucratic authority of the prison. Spontaneous conversations between peers on rights, the lack of rights, and the power of art percolate around the school. For a moment, the class is transformed into a temporary experiment in participatory "abolition democracy" within the prison industrial complex.

—

This book is intended to share that temporary experiment in hopes to keep it alive.

1   Malcolm X, "Racism: The Cancer that Is Destroying America," *Egyptian Gazette*, August 25, 1964, https://www.malcolmx.com/quotes/.

2   Angela Davis, *Abolition Democracy: Beyond Empire, Prisons, and Torture* (New York: Seven Stories Press, 2005), 69-70.

3   Prisoner's Union, *Goals of the Prisoner's Union* (San Francisco: United Prisoner's Union, 1971), http://freedomarchives.org/Documents/Finder/DOC510_scans/United_Prisoners_Union/510.goals.prisoners.union.pdf.

4   "Covid-19's Impact on People in Prison," Equal Justice Initiative, last modified August 21, 2020, https://eji.org/news/covid-19s-impact-on-people-in-prison/.

5   "COVID-19 Cases and Deaths in Federal and State Prisons," Research Letters, JAMA, last modified July 8, 2020, https://jamanetwork.com/journals/jama/fullarticle/2768249.

6   "Covid-19's Impact on People in Prison," Equal Justice Initiative, last modified August 21, 2020, https://eji.org/news/covid-19s-impact-on-people-in-prison/.

Charles McLaurin, *One Feather*, 2016 »

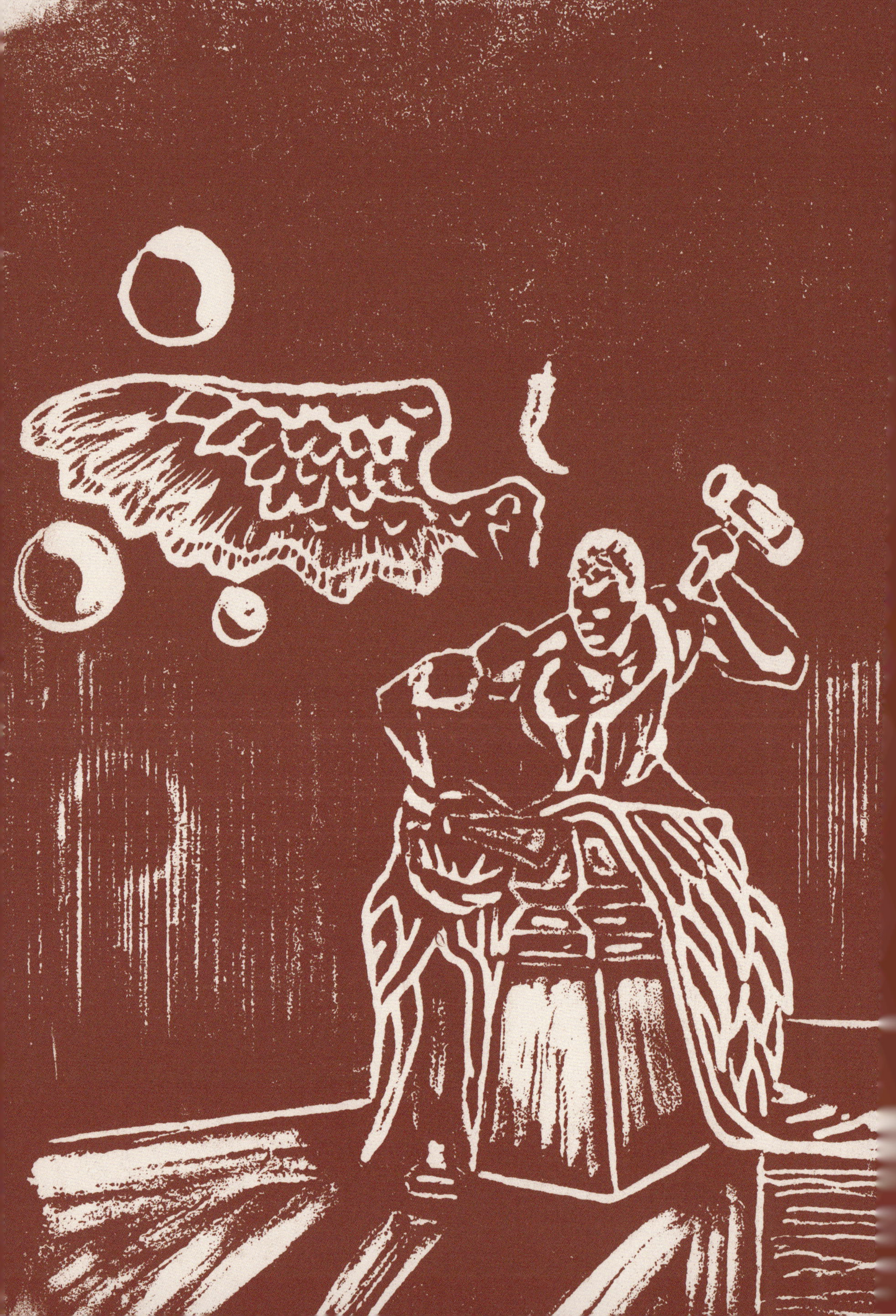

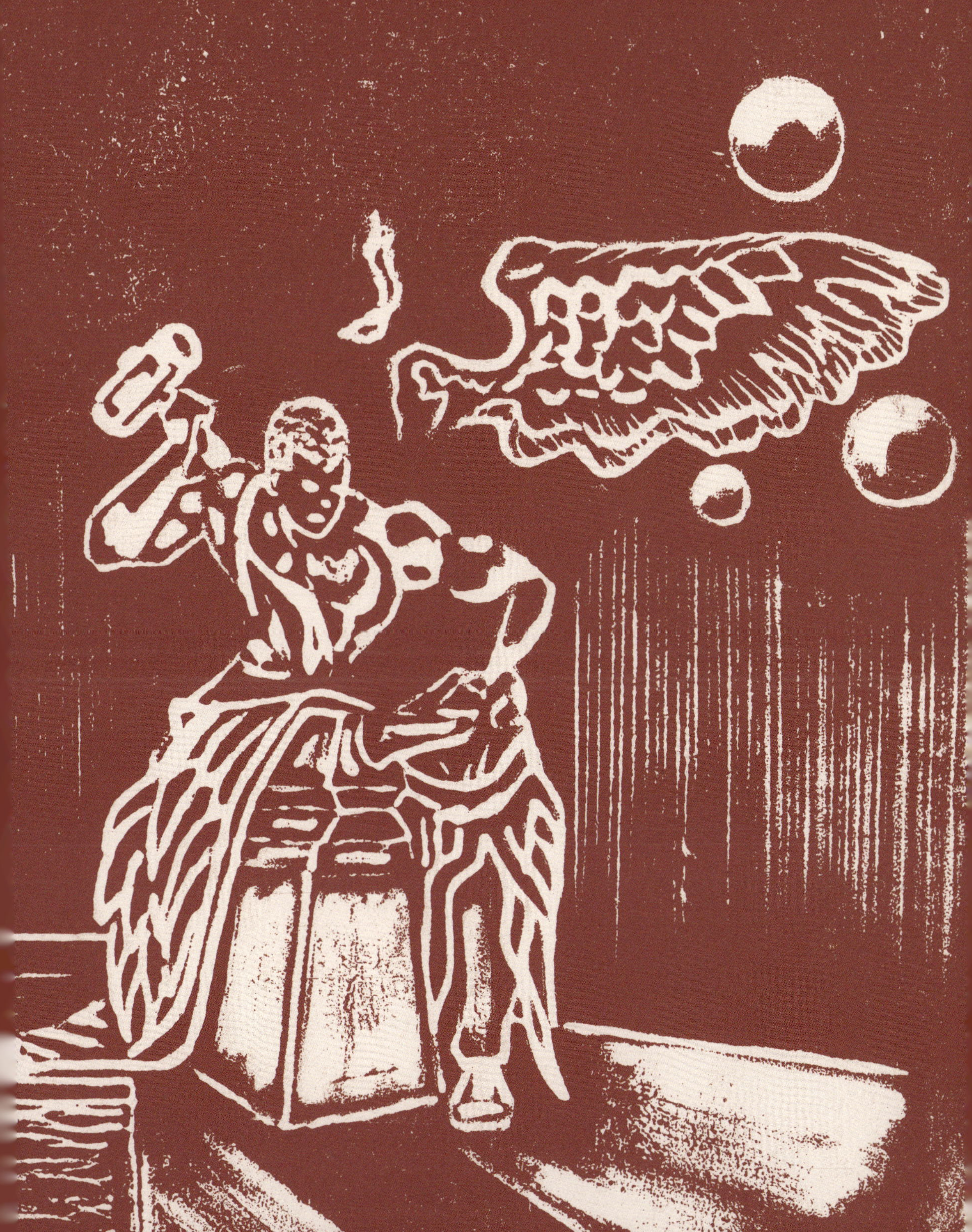

Think, Think

Think about the air invisible as it uncurls
a wave of toxins. Think about how its fingertips
trace the skin as a baton falls on the flesh
merely seconds later. Think about how heavy
metals brown the water and we are told to drink.
Think about how many of us wonder when
the roofs over our heads will be tongues evicted
from the languages of home. Think about how every
person needs a doctor, but everyone doesn't get one.
Think about how savings mean nothing to the crazy
fine print circumscribed like obsolete glyphs. Think
how law books fall open and hopscotch for anyone
who keeps writing checks. Think, think, think like
Aretha Franklin belting what you tryna to do to me?
Think how the law keeps shuffling the numbers to fit
some constant where acknowledging who is human
is posited in some philosophy or some mathematical
equation that pretends that logic is its function, when
blood needs to find something superior, something
that denies how human is defined by a much wider net
cast by some divine fisherman, or perhaps an African
goddess in a gown laced with sea foam, but place markers
for faith are constantly moved toward a crucifix. A human
can find more than one path, I hope. Think about how,
every day, someone is hoping for some simple thing
like fresh bread lightly toasted, the ability to walk without
pain, a chance to shower, a moment free of fist and jeer,
a moment singing victorious as if we could level the wrongs
and leave the world upright, like a gospel-drenched woman
singing freedom, freedom after forgiveness, after you change
your mind, 'cause you need to think (and act) to be free.

American Appetite

Tomorrow,
I'll be at the table
When company comes.
 —Langston Hughes

I, too,
sat at the table of America's Dream Diner,
and raised my hand to order.

What'll you have? asked the weary waitress.

I would like something that tastes like justice, please.
I would like the kneecaps of the officer who knelt
on George Floyd's neck.
(I had been told that the knees were fleshy, fibrous,
soaked to the bone in the last words of George
as he cried for his mother,
steamed in the heat of the surrounding officer's stares
as they mechanically looked away.
I had heard the knee was simmered in the nonchalance
of the officer's hands-in-pocket slouch,
that it would be succulent enough
to make my mouth ring with gospel.)

We are fresh out of kneecaps, sir.
That delivery has been delayed, said the waitress.

I would like a substitute then, please.
I would like the knuckles of the police officers
who fired bullets through twilight
into Breonna Taylor's startled body.
(I had been told that the knuckles would taste like justice,
though they had been pickled in anger and homegrown

in a garden of whispered epithets—
that each crease on each knuckle
was gun-powdered smoky-
sweet with twisted law.)

Sorry, said the waitress, *those
are not on the menu.*

OK.
Well, how about some barbecued
falsely accusing officer fingers, please?
(I had heard they were always in season and so crisp,
so crackling, so well-seasoned—that basted in
brown-faced accusation, they were savory like justice.)

*Sorry, sir, this season has been slow,
and those fingers are slippery hard
to capture.*

Ok, well, how about some
deep fried trigger fingers then?
I'd like some fried 2-seconds-to-shoot-a-12-year-old trigger fingers
with a side of coercive-false-confessions-cop-lips, please.

Sorry, sir.

Perhaps some 19-shot Chicago-style trigger fingers
with a salad of accomplice officers
and mayoral silent tongues?

Maybe tomorrow.

Maybe some country-style KKK trigger fingers,
the ones with Dixie flags on the knuckles and
corporate ink on the fingertips?

Those have never been on our menu, sir.

Tyehimba Jess

Well maybe some feet then—
some cop toes fresh from kicking in warrantless doors
or suspect teeth? A heel well seasoned
in shouts of "Stop resisting."

Sorry, sir, those would be extra-special orders ...

I was running out of patience in America's Dream Diner.
I threw my hands up in frustration.

What kind of American Dream Diner is this anyway?

Where is the napkin stitched from eyelids of cops
looking desperately the other way?

Where is the carafe of intoxicating White Woman Tears
to wash down my gut-shot innocence?

Where is the fork of broken ribs from
death-warrant-signing governors?

Where is the spoon carved from baton
wielding cop wrists hardened with blows
across protester heads?

Where is the bowl of perjurious prosecutor skull
rubbed stainless with its scrub of
plea deal capitalization?

All I wanted to do today was taste a little bit of justice,
and here I am still hungry.

Sir, I have to ask you to lower your voice ... said the waitress.

Seriously?
I see Predator Drone over there feasting
on Yemeni/Afghan bones,
But I can't get one single cop toe?

Sir, please calm ...

I see IMF economic adjustment in back,
feasting on senior citizens' pension plans
on a platter of sweatshop hands
with a whole truckload of refugee sauce,
and I can't get one police knuckle?

And Chevron/Exxon/Haliburton
/Fracking Incorporated over in the corner,
slurping up toddler brains
with a side of grandma liver
on a plate of foreclosed mortgages
and I can't get one kneecap?

But, sir...

Maybe I'm not FalseFlagInaForeignCountry
but I am a citizen of this country,
and is this not *American Dream* Diner?
I came here dreaming of a whiff of justice and ...
Look, sir ...

No, *you* look—
there's No-Knock Arrest over there,
mouth full of molten lead,
with a heaping bowl of Black Body soup.

And what's that over there?
Mouth full of George Washington
stolen slave teeth,
about to slice open a fresh batch of
private prison flesh:
looks like the Presi ...

And then came the Company man.
Security's arm round my throat,
my eyes pitched toward the ceiling,

Tyehimba Jess

my feet flown off the ground,
my head thrown to the floor.

It was only then I remembered
I'd never had the chance to say my grace:

I can't breathe..
I can't breathe..
I can't breathe...
I can't breathe...
I can't breathe...
I can't breathe...
I can't breathe...
I will b r e a t h e. I
can't breathe...
I will b r e a t h e.
I can't breathe...
I will b r e a t h e.
I can't breathe...
I will b r e a t h e.
I will b r e a t h e.
I will b r e a t h e.
I will   BREATHE

I will BREATHE

I AM FIRE

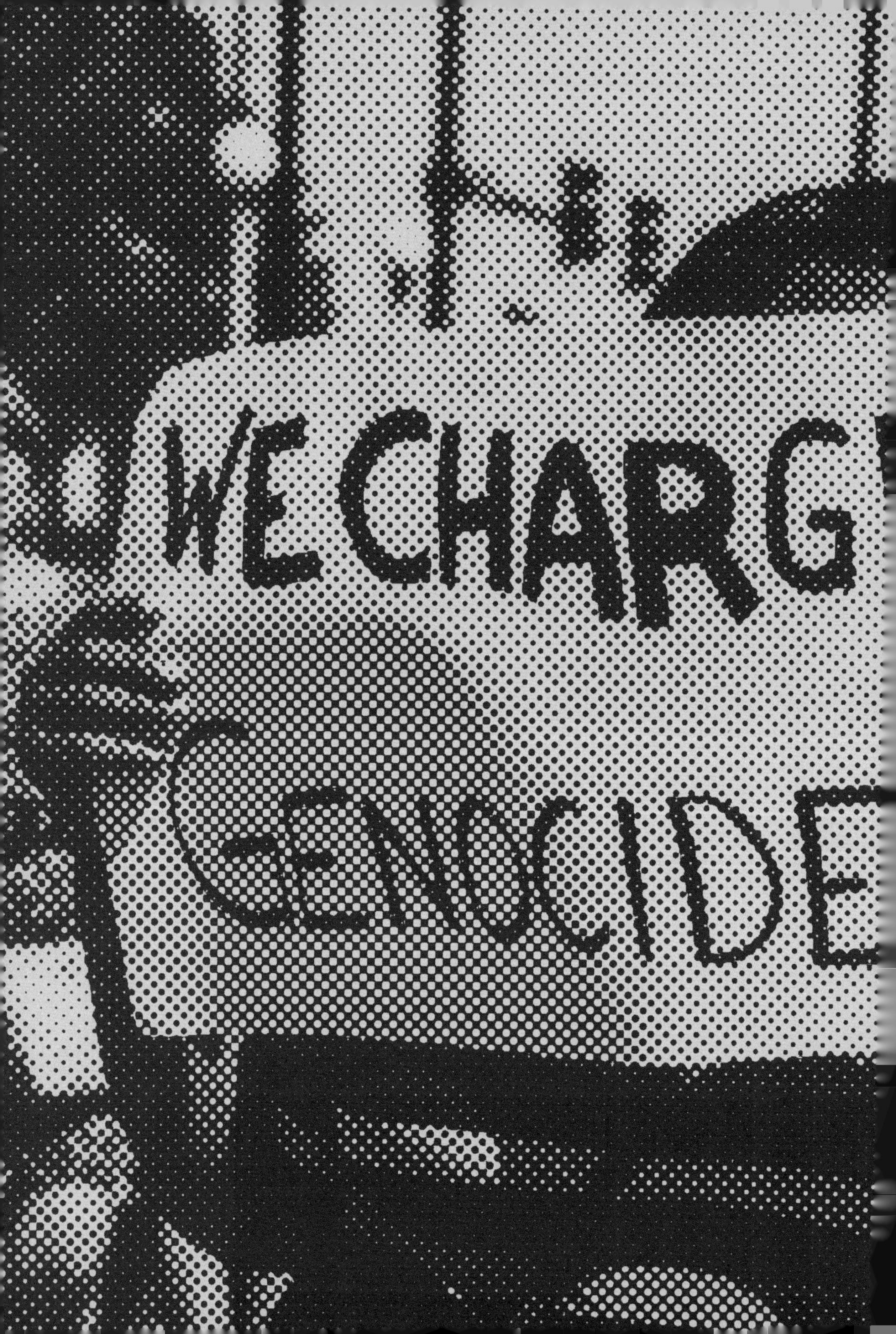

WE CHARG[E]
[G]ENOCIDE

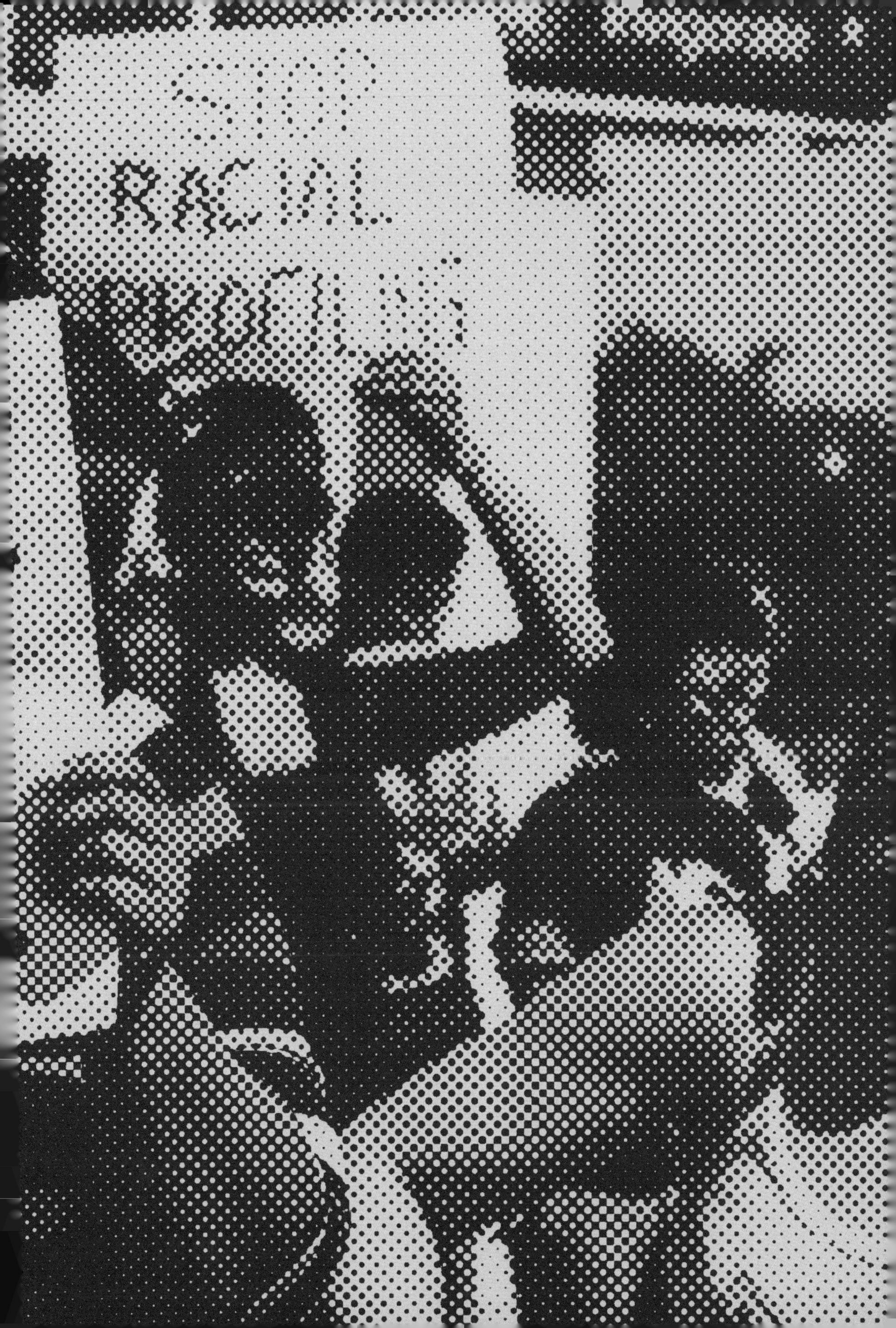

Christophe Ringer

THE FUTURE OF HUMAN RIGHTS

« Photo by Sarah-Ji Rhee, BYP100's Campaign to Decriminalize Black Lives, August 26, 2014

The book that you hold in your hands may well represent the future of human rights. The language of human rights has emerged as a powerful moral and political vocabulary throughout the world. It is often invoked by individuals, organizations, NGO's social justice movements, and nation-states. As the idea of human rights has flourished, so has the reality of their fragility. The moral and spiritual dignity they inspire are often sacrificed for other political, economic, religious, or social interests. Thus, as the idea of human rights has spread, the chorus of critiques has grown louder. For many, human rights are an unredeemable aspect of a colonialism with no respect for deep cultural differences. And to make matters worse, there have been egregious human rights abuses committed in the name of humanitarian intervention. However, there is another story of human rights that is often obscured. It is a story of human rights that emerges from those with very different perspectives and hopes—a story to which the members of Prison + Neighborhood Arts/Education Project (P+NAP) have contributed a powerful chapter. This story is one that was also embraced by Malcolm X, a freedom fighter who was once also incarcerated.

On the evening of April 3rd 1964, Malcolm X delivered an iconic speech, "The Ballot or the Bullet," at Cory Methodist Church in Cleveland at an event sponsored by the Congress for Racial Equality (CORE). It was his fullest articulation of his emerging political philosophy of Black nationalism that crafted a vision of solidarity across ideological and religious divides. In the latter half of the speech, Malcolm X challenges those present not to limit their struggle to the political arena as defined by "Uncle Sam." With his potent mix of fiery rhetoric and razor-sharp logic, he argues, "Civil rights keeps you under his restrictions, under his jurisdiction. Civil rights keep you in his pocket. Civil rights means you're asking Uncle Sam to treat you right ... Human rights are the rights that are recognized by all nations of this earth. And any time anyone violates your human rights, you can take them to the world court."[1] And with those words Malcolm X began actively forging a vision of human rights that would connect the issues facing Blacks in America to other oppressed people in the world fighting for liberation. His vision was to elevate the crimes of America to a world court. Although Malcolm X does not reference it in his speech, he also is building on a legacy that precedes him.

In the shadow of the Second World War, Allied powers gathered in Washington D.C. to develop an organization dedicated to keeping international peace. Commonly known as the Dumbarton Oaks Conference, in October of 1944, American, British, Soviet Union, and Chinese delegations wrestled and negotiated about how to police the world. The issue of human rights struggled to gather support as it was bound by the realities of colonialism abroad and the Jim Crow system of the nation in which the conference was being held.

W.E.B. Du Bois leveled a scathing critique that the proposals coming out of the conference effectively disenfranchised 750 million people and were intolerable, dangerous, and opposed to democracy.[2] The subsequent political and legal maneuvers by the U.S. consistently attempted to avoid the language of human rights. There was palpable fear that if such language entered into the document, the NAACP and Black people could use it to break the grip of Jim Crow.[3] The preservation of American sovereignty in the crafting of the U.N. charter was intimately and inseparably tied to the preservation of Jim Crow. The moral and political contradictions of the U.S. stance, however, provided a small window to make the concrete sufferings of Blacks in America known to the world.

In 1946, the contradiction of America's zeal to prosecute Nazi war criminals and the incompetence and lack of motivation to prosecute domestic terrorism reached a turning point. The State Department itself even recognized that the "Negro problem" had become a "foreign policy problem" that could no longer be ignored.[4] The urgency of the moment was seized by the National Negro Congress (NNC) to do the very thing the U.S. was attempting to prevent—to bring the case of 13 million African Americans into the court of world opinion through the United Nations. The goal of the NNC was to begin to internationalize American racism and frame the political, economic, and social discrimination of Blacks as human rights abuses.

The NNC circulated 100,000 petitions garnering attention with the Black press.[5] The effort faced stiff political resistance. The point that African Americans did not represent a sovereign nation was highlighted in an effort to shield the U.N. from intervening in the domestic affairs of the U.S.[6]

The NNC, however, seized on this opening to forge alliances between African Americans and all people of color under U.S. jurisdiction, such as in Puerto Rico and the Virgin Islands. The goal was to demonstrate that the treatment of Blacks in America fit a pattern of broader U.S. abuses. The effort was downplayed by the larger media and red-baiting charges of communism. As such, the efforts of the NNC eventually dissolved due to organizational and financial challenges. However, there is no doubt that this effort captured the imaginations of Blacks by placing their struggle in an international context. The NAACP in particular was prepared to take up the challenge again.

In 1947, the NAACP produced "An Appeal to the World!" a report on the denial of human rights to Blacks in America. The report, produced under the supervision of W.E.B. Du Bois, was far more comprehensive than the previous effort by the NNC. Eleanor Roosevelt, a board member of the NAACP at the time, was not supportive. She argued that such an effort would be embarrassing to the state department. Unlike the previous effort, the petition caught the attention of the international press. The Black press at home provided wide coverage of the petition. The attention cast an intense light on the problems facing Blacks at home, while America attempted to present itself as a model for democracy before the world. The Soviet Union seized on this opportunity to advance their interests by putting the U.S. on the defense. The systemic injustices suffered by Blacks in America was now known internationally. However, little movement was made on the petition by the U.N. as the politics of the Cold War overshadowed it. Nevertheless, it forced Americans to address the issue before a world audience. A new strategy for those pursuing social justice became real.

In 1948, after several years of debate, the U.N. finally approved the Convention on the Prevention and Punishment of the Crime of Genocide. The language of the convention would eventually provide an opening to address racial injustice. The convention defined genocide as acts with the "intent to destroy, in whole or in part, a national, ethnical, racial, or religious group."[7] The specific acts covered in the convention include: 1) killing members of the group; 2) causing serious bodily or mental harm to its members; 3) deliberately inflicting on the group conditions of life calculated to bring about its physical destruction in whole or in part; 4) imposing measures intended to prevent births within the group; and 5) forcibly transferring children of the group to another group. William L. Patterson, the national secretary of the Civil Rights Congress (CRC), began to see the possibilities of addressing racial justice through this convention. Patterson, a prominent activist known for his leadership in the Scottsboro Nine case, had experience in advocating at the U.N. on behalf of individuals. Patterson now recognized an opportunity to address Black people as a group.

In 1951 William Patterson stepped off of a plane in Paris and personally delivered "We Charge Genocide: The Crime of Government Against the Negro People" to the United Nations Committee on Human Rights. The report spanned 200 pages with extensive accounts of racial murders and state-sanctioned executions, including 152 incidences of unarmed Black men and women killed by police or lynch mobs. The petition gathered the evidence from a vast array of sources, such as Black presses, colleges, and advocacy organizations, as well as city, state, and federal agencies. The petition convincingly takes advantage of two aspects of the U.N.'s definition of genocide. The first is that genocide need not be total but "in part" and included the imposition of life conditions which lead to the premature destruction in whole or in part of a people. As such, in addition to the accounts of killing, the petition charges America with "Economic Genocide."[8] This term brought into view the way Blacks suffered from greater rates of infant mortality, disease, inadequate medical care, and education, as well as shorter life spans. Previous petitions to the United Nations were consistently caught in the dilemma of sovereignty. Since African Americans did not constitute a nation, it was difficult to move the U.N. to act. Patterson's novel approach of using the conventions around genocide set the issue on new moral ground and captured international attention.

Although the petition captured international attention, the political climate was particularly oppressive for Patterson given his association with communism. In the midst of the Red Scare, authorities used Patterson's refusal to provide the names of members and donors of the CRC to incarcerate him. The influence of the petition would not be forgotten. In 2014, a grassroots inter-generational volunteer movement began to center the voices and experiences of young people of color targeted by police and who experienced police violence in Chicago. The name of the group is We Charge Genocide, in recognition of Patterson's pioneering efforts. A new generation of activists generated a report revealing a pattern of torture by the Chicago Police Department (CPD) in Violation of Articles 2, 10, 11, 12, 13, and 14 of the Convention of Torture at the United Nations. The report documented incidents and statistics on harassment and abuse, use of excessive force, deadly force, sexual assaults, mass arrest, and detention. The group traveled to the UN in Geneva to expose the persistence of police violence in

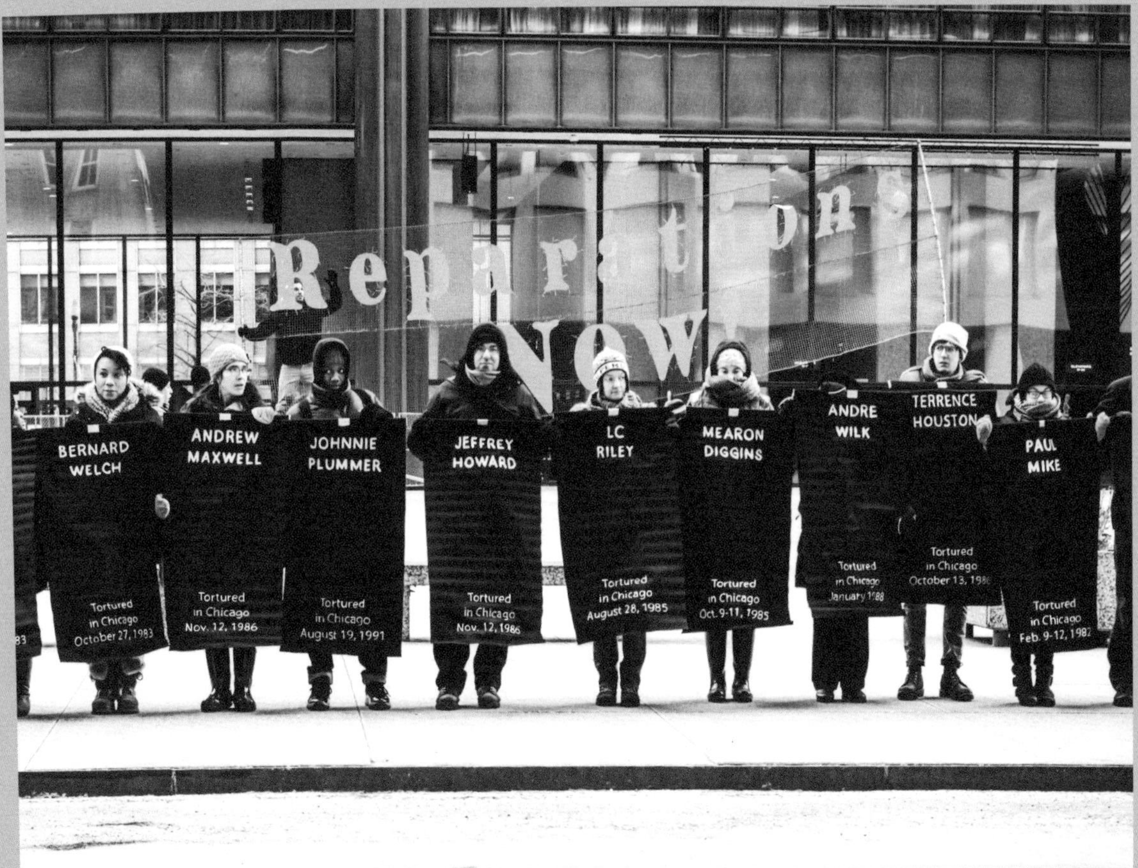

Chicago. In addition, they pressed for reparations and staged silent protest.[9] We Charge Genocide provided creativity and the strong voices of young people in a movement with organizations such as Chicago Torture Justice Memorials, Project NIA and the ACLU that passed a historic reparations package to survivors of police torture in Chicago.

One of the ugliest chapters in the history of violence by the Chicago Police Department is the reign of Commander Jon Burge. Burge ran a team that tortured at least 125 Black victims using electric shocks, beatings, burnings, and suffocation from 1972 to 1991.[10] This history is extensively chronicled in Flint Taylor's *The Torture Machine: Racism and Police Violence.* One important aspect from this human rights campaign to highlight here is that Burge, a product of a predominantly white enclave on Chicago's South Side, served in Vietnam prior to becoming a police officer. There is evidence that it was there, as a member of the Ninth Military Police Company, that he learned techniques of torture.[11] In 2004, Standish Willis, a community activist and civil rights attorney, watched as America was forced to respond to condemnation from across the world for the torture at Abu Ghraib. Recognizing the parallels, he decided to take these experiences of torture worldwide.[12] Willis founded the group Black People Against Torture and presented evidence of Chicago's torture squad to the Organization of American State's Inter-American Commission on Human Rights in 2005. Their legacy gave ground for an extraordinary range of survivors, activists, organizers, attorneys, and artists from Chicago Torture Justice Memorials, We Charge Genocide, Project NIA, and the ACLU to organize for and win reparations for survivors of torture under Burge's reign. They won $5.5 million in reparations on May 6, 2015 from the Chicago City Council.

This brief account of human rights from the underside of history demonstrates a profound tenacity to hang on to an ideal and vision of human dignity. At critical times this vision was hampered by philosophical, cultural, legal, and political challenges. This historic case of securing reparations represents a foreshadowing of the meaning of human rights to come. The campaign for reparations did not stop at a monetary recognition. Included in this vision is a series of reparative projects: a center for counseling and support for torture survivors (the first in the nation of its kind), a memorial, and a mandatory curriculum about the cases in Chicago Public Schools. This is a vision of repairing harm that addresses the survivors, their families, and a city's collective memory.

This campaign demonstrates that if human rights have a meaningful future in alleviating social miseries and ending human rights violations, it will be because a culture of human rights has been developed. This means cultural, civic, religious, and governmental organizations must embrace the idea of human rights from below, which entails hearing the voices of those whose human rights have been violated. It is these voices that help discern the true meaning of human rights.

A powerful example of this is the art of Darrell W. Fair, a Burge torture survivor. Darrell offers a compelling artistic rendering of Article 11 that establishes the presumption of innocence and a fair trial as a human right. Darrell's rendering weaves the abstract legal language of the Universal Declaration of Human Rights (UDHR) with the concrete pain and suffering of police violence. It is palpable. Like so many powerful works of art, Darrell's print expresses his own experience, along with so many others. His art captures the suffering and violence documented in *We Charge Genocide* and

The Torture Machine. As I write these words, it's impossible to look at Darrell's art and not see Officer Derek Chauvin killing a handcuffed George Floyd by holding his knee on Floyd's neck until he's no longer able to breathe. This is the kind of art that reminds us why a culture of human rights is so desperately needed. The book you hold in your hands is a step forward in building it.

---

1. Malcolm X, "The Ballot or The Bullet," in *Malcolm X Speaks: Selected Speeches and Statements*, ed. George Brietman (New York: Grove Press, 1990), 23.

2. Carol Anderson, *Eyes Off the Prize: The United Nations and the African American Struggle for Human Rights, 1944-1965* (New York: Cambridge University Press), 38.

3. Anderson, *Eyes Off the Prize*, 44.

4. Anderson, *Eyes Off the Prize*, 74.

5. Charles Martin, "Internationalizing 'The American Dilemma': The Civil Rights Congress and the 1951 Genocide Petition to the United States," *Journal of American Ethnic History* 16(4): 35-61.

6. Martin, "Internationalizing," 88.

7. "U.N. Convention on the Prevention and Punishment of the Crime of Genocide," United Nations, accessed November 20, 2020, https://www.un.org/en/genocideprevention/documents/atrocity-crimes/Doc.1_Convention%20on%20the%20Prevention%20and%20Punishment%20of%20the%20Crime%20of%20Genocide.pdf.

8. William Patterson, Ed. *The Civil Rights Congress. We Charge Genocide: The Historic Petition to the United Nations for Relief From a Crime of the United States Government Against the People* (New York: Civil Rights Congress, 1970), 5.

9. Flint Taylor, *The Torture Machine: Racism and Police Violence in Chicago* (Chicago: Haymarket Books, 2019), 467.

10. Natalie Y. Moore, "Payback," *The Marshall Project*, October 30, 2018, https://www.themarshallproject.org/2018/10/30/payback.

11. John Conroy, "Tools of Torture," *Chicago Reader*, February 3, 2005, https://www.chicagoreader.com/chicago/tools-of-torture/Content?oid=917876.

12. Moore, "Payback."

Darrell Wayne Fair, *UDHR Article 11* (Detail), 2018 »

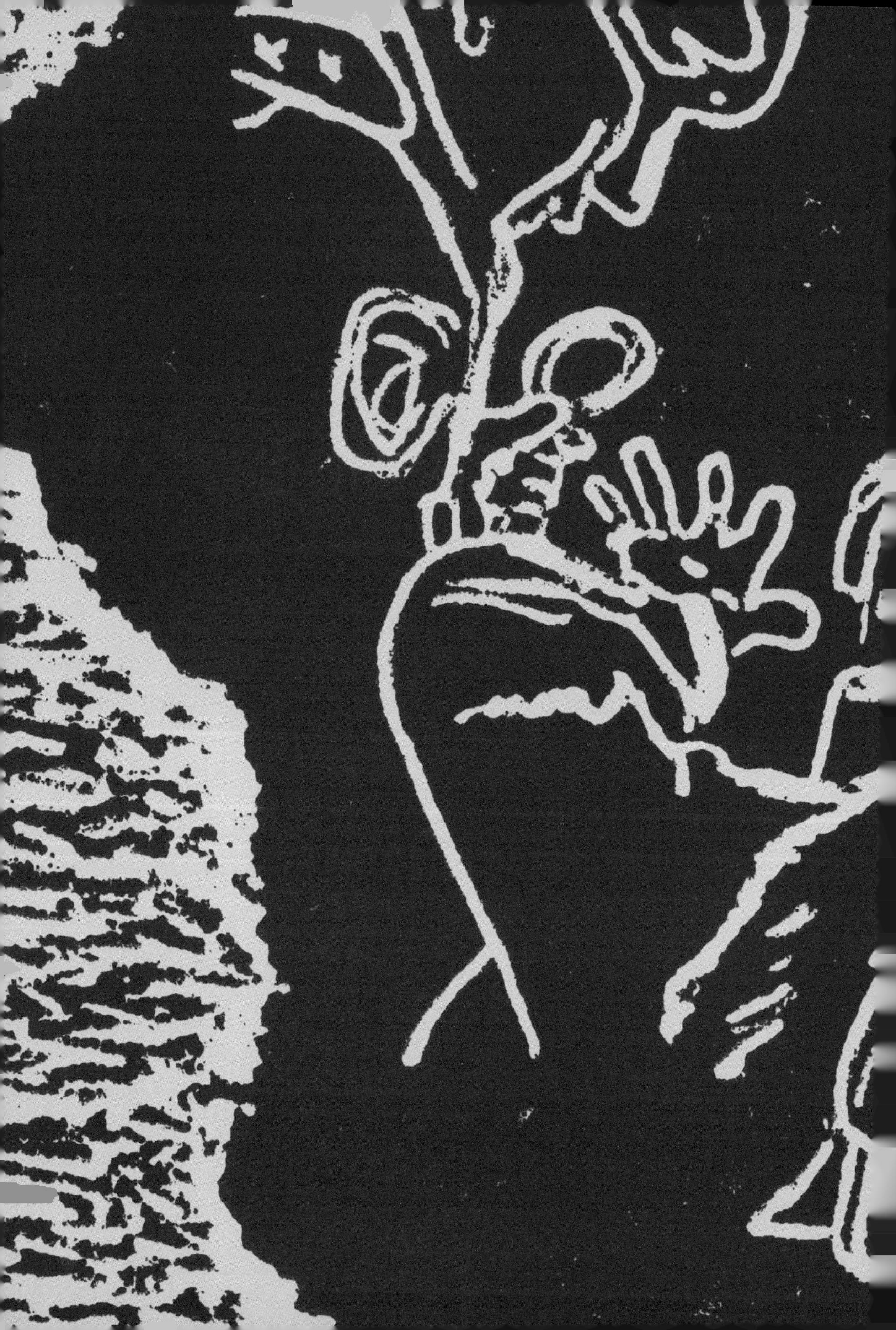

To Be Human

To be human is to admit; I am flawed; with the
capacity to do unimaginable harm.
We can create wonder, destructive means to
Kill and maim each other.
Some of us can produce the most vile, virulent strains
Of hate on Earth;
Just ask the shade of its latest victim
Ahmaud Arbery. Who for no other reason than the
Color of his skin.
He was judged to be not human, stalked and killed
Like an animal.

As I stand in the nebulous rays of dawn,
I question MY humanity.
How long will my people suffer this humiliation
With forced humility!?!
Content to let "White Daddy" deal with all
our problems.

I scream, yell; I cry out "Why LORD!"
"Why have you forsaken us!?!"
Forsaken me?! To be consumed by this
xenophobic ecosystem;
Envenom; nursing my loathing; My blood
quickens!! Bedlam!!

But there's an eerie ebb and flow
To being human,
it's easy to justify the cannibalizing
of one's soul.
To be human? Least to me; is to embrace the
multifaceted aspects of our humanity.

Look past all the emotional deformities.
You don't have to love me, but at least
understand.
That we may be different; but; Damn it!!
I'm still a Human!!
I stand in defiance of those who would
view with horror my humanity;
Since birth they branded me; deemed me unworthy;

Love, compassion, and understanding are
important components to being Human;
Understanding that even though Humanity is
vast and diverse. If we work together we can
achieve great things.

Having compassion for those who have less
than; help pull them up and out of a world that's
been run amok.

Show love and admiration; Rejoice for we
finally have reconciliation!!
Can You imagine that? Nice Dream.
To be Human? Guess that's in the eye of the beholder...

Nikki Patin

Shout from the Distance

The air always smells wet
The bread always looks dry
There is never any physical contact
Every hall, every wall evokes distance
Forced to gather together
Some choose to remain apart

We thrive on remaining apart
Even though everyone's blood is wet
No one wants to be forced together
Wells stay running dry
No longer yearn to bridge any distance
Generations of compelled contact

Leaves us resenting further contact
I like you better when we're apart
Isn't that the shout from the distance?
Throats parched in the shadow of your wet?
You understand the cruelty of dry
But even that can't bring us together

Everybody sick of together
How we infect each other on contact
Eyes empty and dry
Relentless in our pursuit of apart, apart
Whose heart can stay wet
When even blood can't go the distance?

How far is the distance
From resentment to together
When too many faces are wet
Bloodied and buried on contact

Love and self kept profitably apart
All bitter and broken and dry

Even the sky is dry
How soothing the disassociated distance
This is how you keep us apart
Spirits wrestling to come together
Didn't we come here to make contact?
To understand these levels of wet?

Fear that drives us apart, dry
Chasing wet across the distance
All we got is together; no revolution without contact

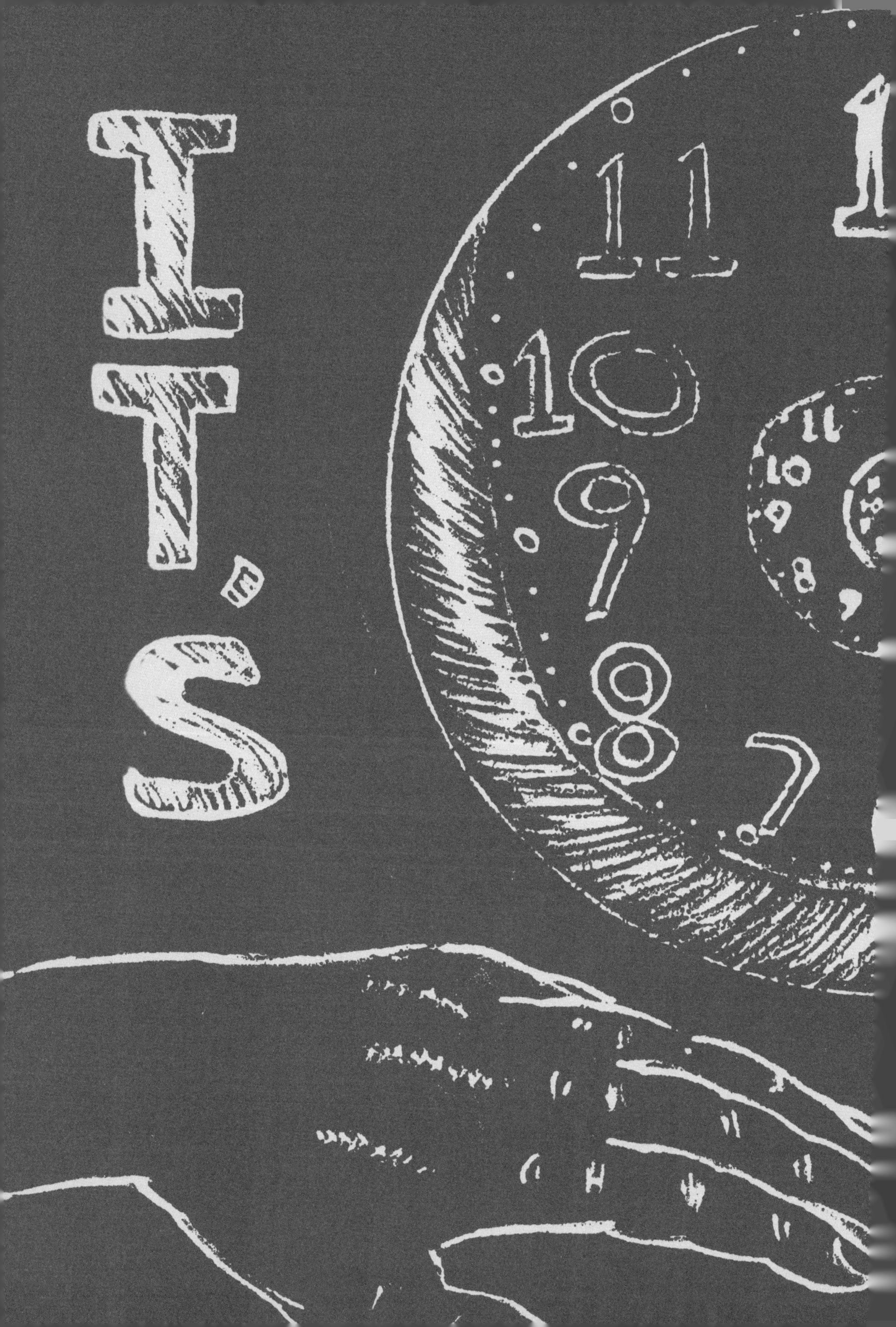
IT'S

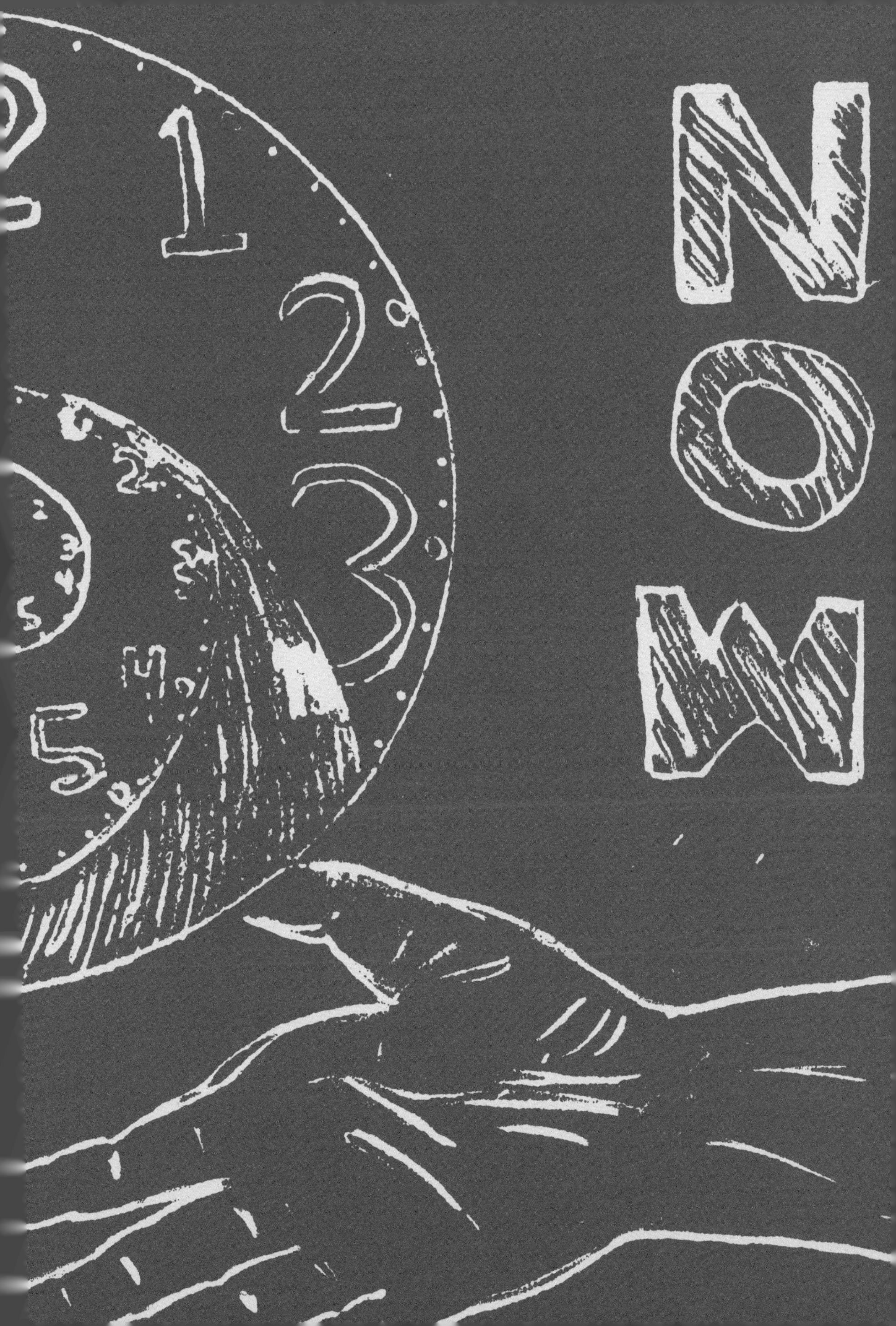
N
O
W

Darrell Wayne Fair

RIGHTS, NOT A PRIVILEGE

« Darrell Wayne Fair, *It's Now*, 2016

Human rights are a right, not a privilege.

I am human which makes me entitled to the right to live and to thrive. Yet, as an African-American and since 1619, when my ancestors, the first of 12.5 million people forced into the transatlantic slave trade, set foot at Point Comfort, Virginia, my people have yet to obtain equal and human rights. Those first 20 to 30 slaves arriving to this land didn't obtain them. And more than 400 years later, in 2020, George Floyd certainly didn't obtain them. He complied and didn't resist, he repeatedly told Officer Chauvin that he couldn't breathe, he struggled to adjust his head into a position that would allow air to enter into his lungs, and in desperation called out for his deceased mother as the air slowly drained from his lungs.

In 1998, the 50th anniversary of the Universal Declaration of Human Rights, my own life intersected with the police. My experience was not as tragic as Mr. Floyd's encounter, but it was an experience that far too many people of color have had to endure. I was illegally arrested from my home and taken to Area 2 police station, located on the South Side of Chicago, a station known for the torture and abuse of individuals in police custody by Jon Burge and those under his command. I was chained to a metal ring on the wall, I wasn't given my asthma inhaler, I was repeatedly kicked and threatened with a gun. I was verbally and mentally abused, not allowed to call family or a lawyer, and for over 30 hours, I had no access to the bathroom, no food, and no sleep. It ended when I agreed to give a verbal statement, followed by the state's attorney writing my name on the signature line to waive my rights.

Ironically, for me, the civil courts are the only avenues available to seek systemic changes. Malcolm X juxtaposed civil rights with human rights and noted the limitations and servitude associated with civil rights versus the emancipatory benefits of human rights. He saw human rights as a form of global recognition, which is exactly what we've been seeing with the global support and solidarity for George Floyd and the Black Lives Matter movement.

With this in mind, the Universal Declaration of Human Rights offers three articles that are particularly important to me. Article 4 outlaws slavery and servitude in all their forms. As a person of color, my humanity has been impacted by slavery. Its evil is visible where white supremacy has systemically and structurally produced inequality. We see the legacy of slavery in zoning and housing policy, access to healthcare, criminal justice policy, access to quality education, and opportunities for employment. This is also important because, even now, as I fight to regain my freedom from my wrongful conviction, I've endured almost 23 years of forced servitude in prison, which is addressed in Article 23. Finally, Article 25 is essential—it does a beautiful job of succinctly stating the basic rights that every human being is entitled to, mandatory essentials for a humane quality of life. This article articulates the human rights that are so important to people at Stateville Prison, where I am currently locked up. Here, many of our human rights have been or are being violated. The living conditions are inhumane. We are housed like chattel in overcrowded facilities that are underfunded and unsustainable. The infrastructure is deteriorating and not maintained. Windows are missing and/or broken; there are insect and rodent infestations; the water is tainted with radium; the food isn't nutritious; and the health care system delays treatments, does not offer follow up appointments, has difficulty getting approvals from outside experts and more. There's forced servitude, unequal pay for labor and inflated costs for services and commissary items. Many of us are here due to targeted criminalization or other forms of systemic racism, such as disproportionate sentences or inadequate legal representation.

To counter these injustices, we use our voice and we litigate, which brings awareness and changes in policy and conditions. It is very important for people at Stateville to demand justice. First of all, when you give voice and a face to an injustice, you bring awareness, you educate and inform. Throughout our history, people both in and out of prison have demanded justice and human rights. This is still true today, especially for the members of the Stateville community. We know change doesn't come unless it is demanded, power seldom concedes willingly.

It is important to note that these demands for human rights from prison and, more broadly, from the bottom up only begin to disentangle the problematic historic relationship between human rights and state violence. The Universal Declaration of Human Rights was crafted by United Nations member states, many of which had histories of colonialism, slavery, and exploitation.

This is why it is essential that the struggle for human rights be led by the people most impacted by state violence and other forms of oppression. Who best to listen to and hear from than those who have lived these experiences?

In Christophe Ringer's essay, included in this compilation, he writes that to alleviate social miseries and end human rights violations, we'll need to develop "a culture of human rights... this entails hearing the voices of those whose human rights have been violated." Since the police killing of George Floyd, there has been an acknowledgment in the public sphere that white supremacy lies at the root of systemic racism. In this current, transformative movement for human rights and racial justice, I see three important things at work that might start to dismantle white supremacy and create a culture of human rights: empathy, education, and action. The protestors show a diversity, compassion, and genuine empathy for those impacted. They look to education to create awareness and acknowledgment of historical truths, causes of injustice, and solutions for change. The protests have renewed a culture of generative action that urges new policy and legislation in local, state, and federal governments. They also have targeted corporations demanding divestment from racist and inequitable companies and investment in Black and Brown futures. The recent dismantling of monuments, the ban on displays of the Dixie flag, the renaming of popular brands and sports teams are a direct response—finally—to the voices of people most targeted and harmed by those symbols: these are all examples of the "development of a culture of human rights" being shaped right now.

A new culture of human rights will inculcate our consciousness, one that was misshapen from this nation's start. Our founding fathers drafted our constitution, which contains 84 clauses, six of which deal directly with slavery and enslaved people. In five more clauses there are implications of slavery. The popular imagination in the U.S. was not only molded by propaganda and racial science—the ideology was also upheld by laws, enforced by the Supreme Court's 1857 Dred Scott decision, for instance. The ruling held that all Black people, enslaved or not, come from a slave race, which made them inferior to white people. The Court stated that the "negro race" was a "separate class of people" and has "no rights which a white man was bound to respect." This is the language of racism and white supremacy that lingers today. We need to eradicate from our popular imagination this divisive language and ideology. Building off the Universal Declaration of Human Rights, we must heed the voices and demands of those most impacted and develop a "culture of human rights" in order to ensure that human rights *are* a right, not a privilege.

Charles McLaurin, The Protest, 2016 »

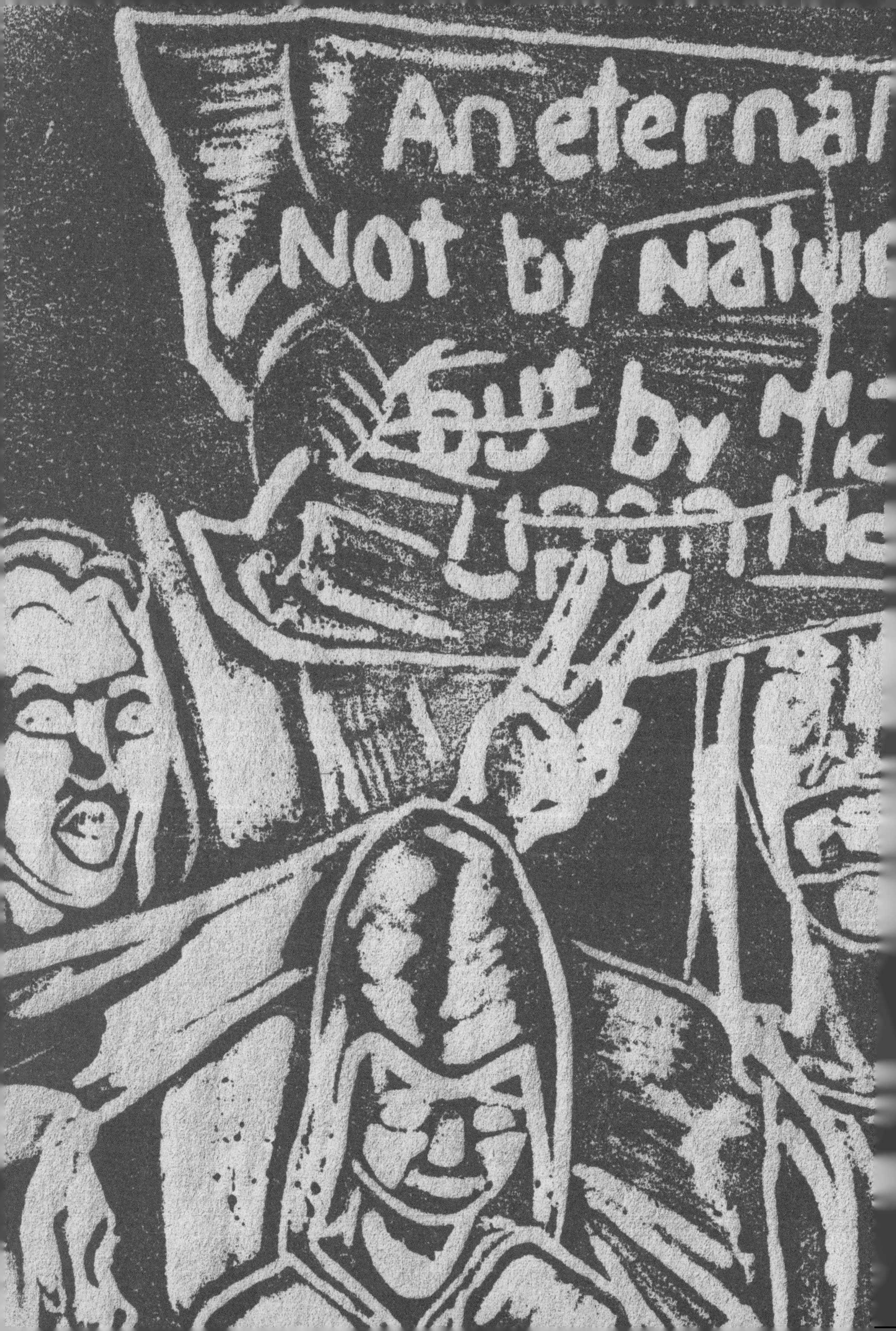

An eternal
Not by Natu
but by M

uffering
s ykrat

Eric Blackmon

I AM EQUAL

I am equal.
I am no longer chattel.
I haven't been born or bred for nobody's use.
I don't belong to nobody.
I am not anybody's slave.

I am equal.
I am not three-fifths.
I am not second class.
I am not to be segregated.
Degraded.
Berated.
Subservient
Or Submissive.
I am not worthless.

I am equal.
I will not be silenced.
I will not be overlooked.
I will not be cast aside.
I am not invisible.

I am equal.
I am strong. Stronger now than ever.
I am smart. Smarter than you've ever imagined.
I am here.
Forever.
To be heard.
To be felt.
To be respected.
To be seen.
I AM EQUAL!

Mountains with Rugs on Top of Them!

When the first ships arrived here, Old
Chris took their hospitality and turned on
them. Bringing all types of disease, raping
their queens, and slaughtering their kids,
stealing their land and they called the Indians
the savages!! "Stop playing" (sweep) kidnap, yeah kidnap.
They stole Black men from their Motherland,
stealing our culture, robbing us of ours.
Identify (sweep) slavery, rape and hanging of Black people (sweep)
Hundreds of years of cruelty, then followed
by racism, segregation, and plain hatred
(sweep) Japanese Americans put in camps
(pretty much prison) for just being Japanese,
Blacks, women, and all minorities not having
any rights! (sweep) The killing of Black
civil rights leaders, underfunded schools,
violating our constitutional rights and Jim Crow
laws (sweep) police brutality, pushing cocaine
in our community to fund wars and thousands
of other savage acts on the underprivileged.
Them not mountains with rugs on top of them.
That's Amerika, they then sweep so much dirt
under them rugs, them rugs then turn into
mountains with rugs on top
of them!!

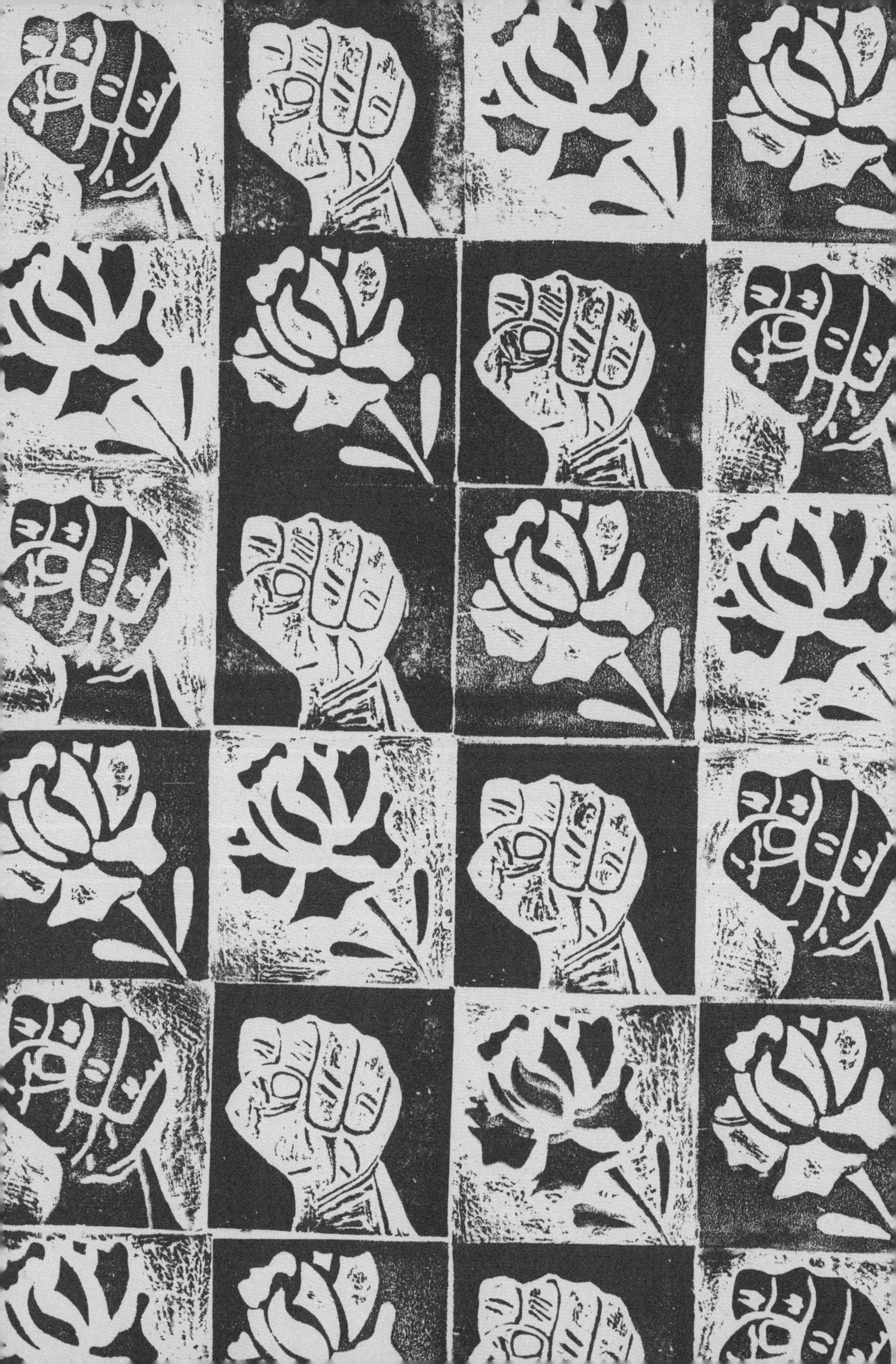

UNIVERSAL DECLARATION OF HUMAN RIGHTS

THE UNIVERSAL DECLARATION
OF HUMAN RIGHTS

*The Universal Declaration of Human Rights (UDHR) is a milestone
document in the history of human rights. Drafted by representatives
with different legal and cultural backgrounds from all regions of
the world, the Declaration was proclaimed by the United Nations
General Assembly in Paris on 10 December 1948 (General Assembly
resolution 217 A) as a common standard of achievement for all
peoples and all nations. It sets out, for the first time, fundamental
human rights to be universally protected and it has been translated
into over 500 languages.*[1]

Featured here are foam block prints for each of the 30 Articles of the UDHR
created by artists at Stateville Prison. While reflecting the challenges of
image-making in prison conditions, the designs are the start of a conversation
about what it means to represent justice and carve out rights from inside the
prison industrial complex. Collectively the prints reject the conditional rights
and dehumanization perpetuated by the carceral state and claim the dignity of
universal inalienable rights. The print series was inspired by Meredith Stern's
Universal Declaration of Human Rights Print Project and was developed in
a class taught by Aaron Hughes through the Prison + Neighborhood Arts/
Education Project in 2018.

Whereas recognition of the inherent dignity and of the equal and inalienable rights of all members of the human family is the foundation of freedom, justice and peace in the world,

Whereas disregard and contempt for human rights have resulted in barbarous acts which have outraged the conscience of mankind, and the advent of a world in which human beings shall enjoy freedom of speech and belief and freedom from fear and want has been proclaimed as the highest aspiration of the common people,

Whereas it is essential, if man is not to be compelled to have recourse, as a last resort, to rebellion against tyranny and oppression, that human rights should be protected by the rule of law,

Whereas it is essential to promote the development of friendly relations between nations,

Whereas the peoples of the United Nations have in the Charter reaffirmed their faith in fundamental human rights, in the dignity and worth of the human person and in the equal rights of men and women and have determined to promote social progress and better standards of life in larger freedom,

Whereas Member States have pledged themselves to achieve, in co-operation with the United Nations, the promotion of universal respect for and observance of human rights and fundamental freedoms,

Whereas a common understanding of these rights and freedoms is of the greatest importance for the full realization of this pledge,

Now, Therefore THE GENERAL ASSEMBLY proclaims THIS UNIVERSAL DECLARATION OF HUMAN RIGHTS as a common standard of achievement for all peoples and all nations, to the end that every individual and every organ of society, keeping this Declaration constantly in mind, shall strive by teaching and education to promote respect for these rights and freedoms and by progressive measures, national and international, to secure their universal and effective recognition and observance, both among the peoples of Member States themselves and among the peoples of territories under their jurisdiction.

---

1   "Universal Declaration of Human Rights," United Nations, accessed September 1, 2019, https://www.un.org/en/universal-declaration-human-rights/.

64|65

Article 1.

All human beings are born free and equal in dignity and rights. They are endowed with reason and conscience and should act towards one another in a spirit of brotherhood.

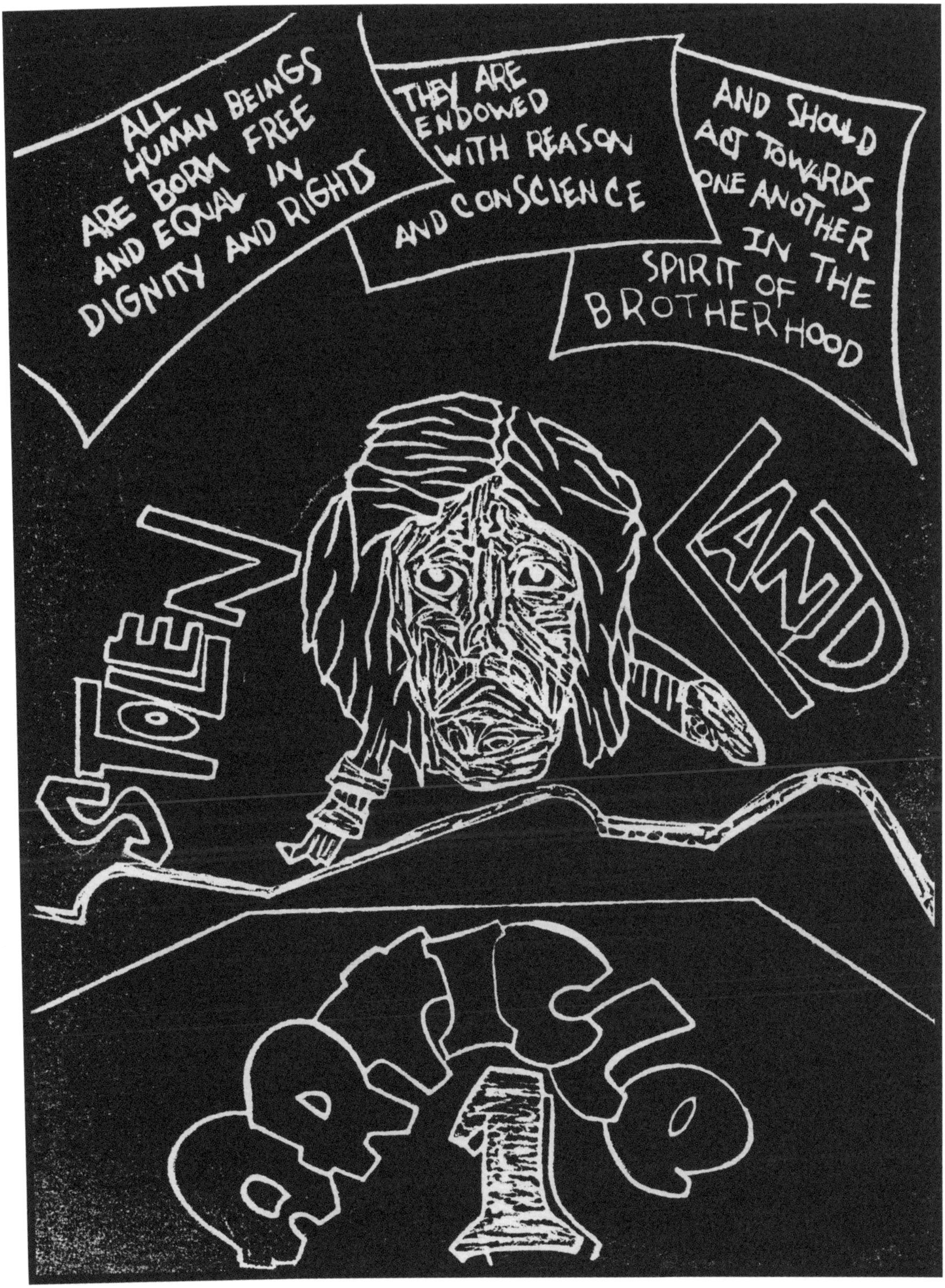

ALL HUMAN BEINGS ARE BORN FREE AND EQUAL IN DIGNITY AND RIGHTS
THEY ARE ENDOWED WITH REASON AND CONSCIENCE
AND SHOULD ACT TOWARDS ONE ANOTHER IN THE SPIRIT OF BROTHERHOOD
STOLEN
LAND

Article 2.

Everyone is entitled to all the rights and freedoms set forth in this
Declaration, without distinction of any kind, such as race, colour, sex,
language, religion, political or other opinion, national or social origin,
property, birth or other status. Furthermore, no distinction shall be made
on the basis of the political, jurisdictional or international status of the
country or territory to which a person belongs, whether it be independent,
trust, non-self-governing or under any other limitation
of sovereignty.

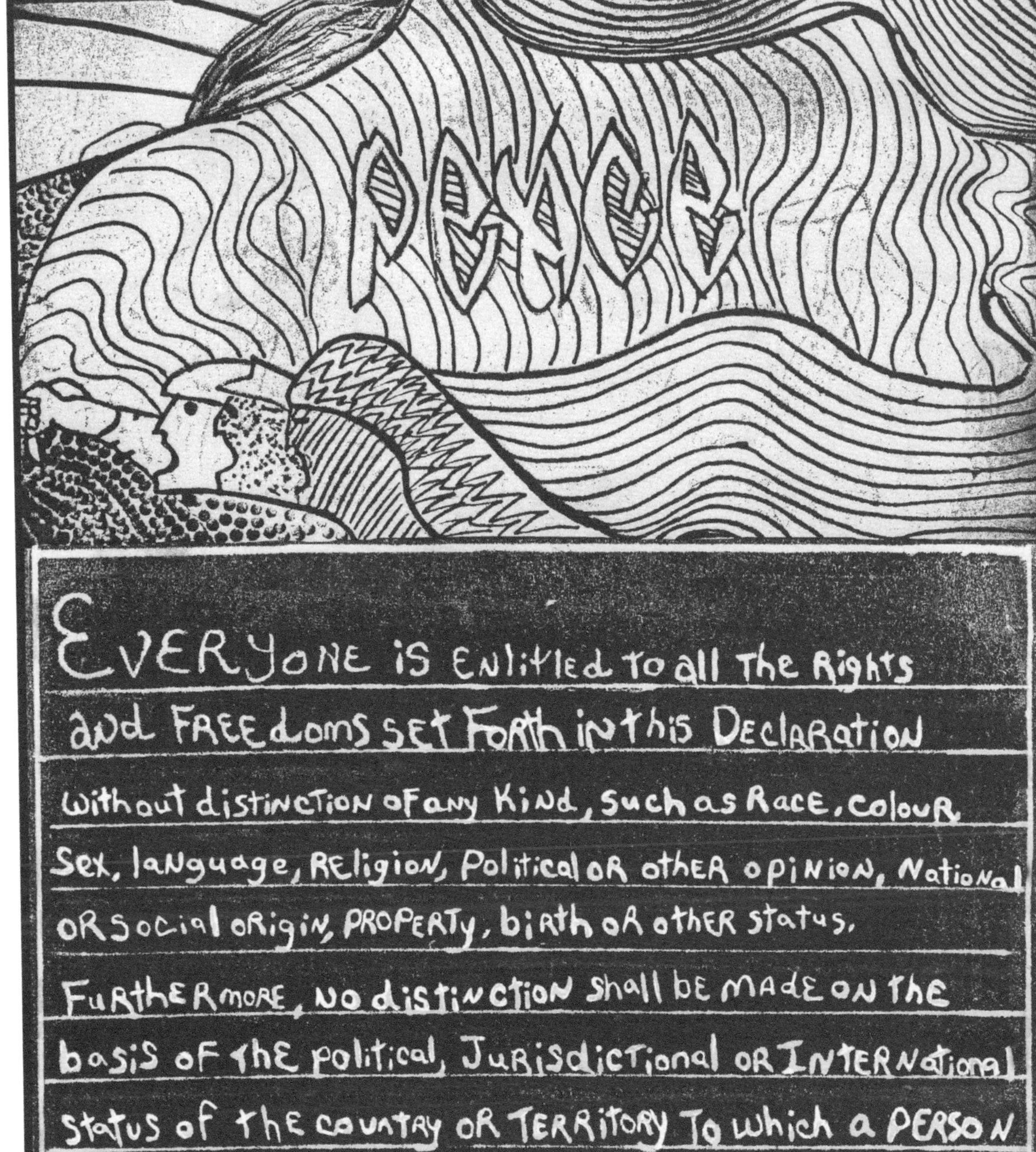
PEACE
EVERYONE is entitled to all the Rights
and FREEdoms set Forth in this Declaration
without distinction of any kind, such as Race, colour,
Sex, language, Religion, Political or other opinion, National
or Social origin, PROPERTY, birth or other status.
FurtherMore, no distinction shall be made on the
basis of the political, Jurisdictional or INTERNational
status of the country or TERRitory To which a PERSON
belongs, whether it be Independent, TRUST, NON-
self-governing or under any other limitation
of sovereignty.

Article 3.

Everyone has the right to life, liberty and security of person.

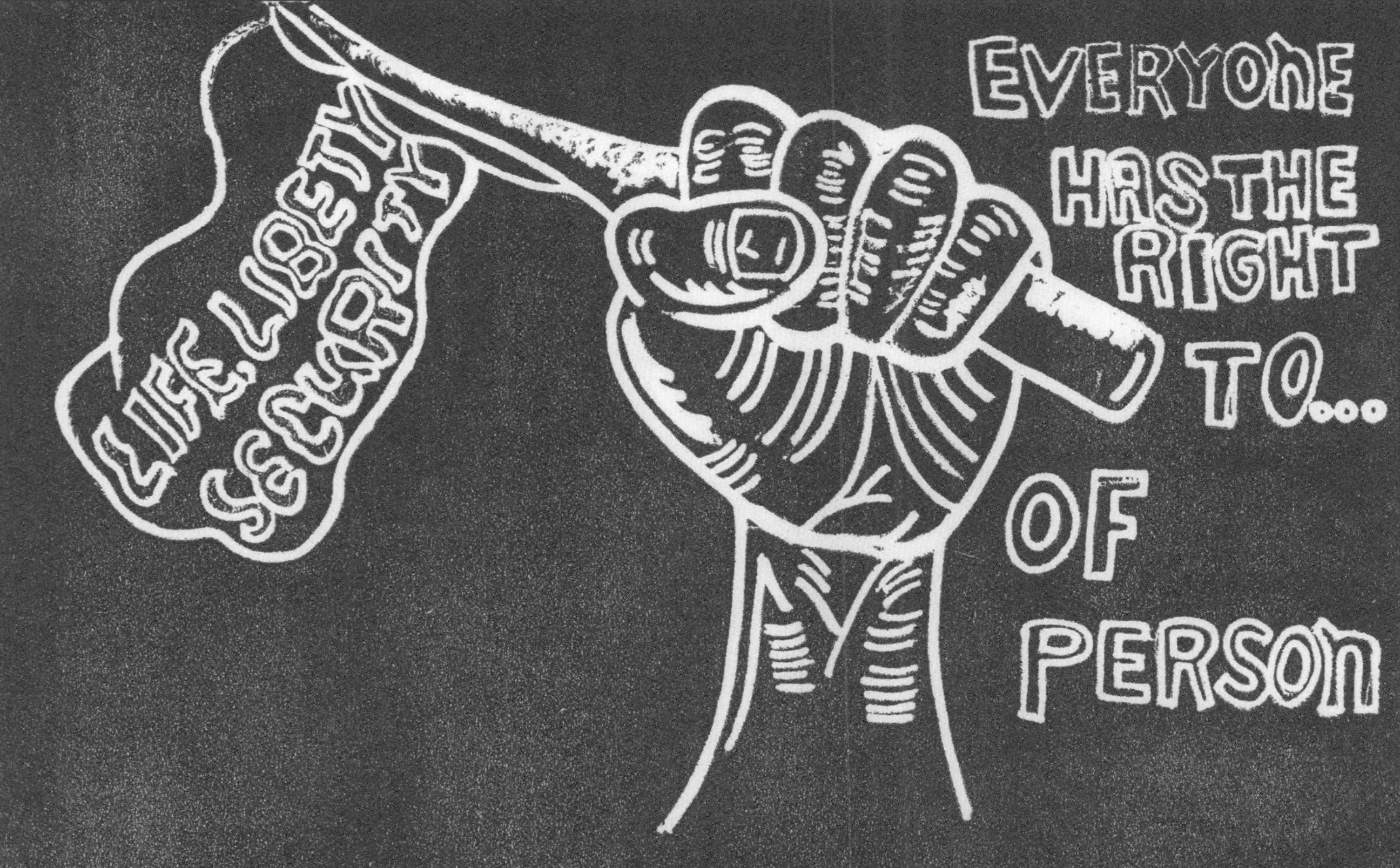

EVERYONE HAS THE RIGHT TO...
OF PERSON
LIFE, LIBETY SECURITY

Article 4.

No one shall be held in slavery or servitude; slavery and the slave trade shall be prohibited in all their forms.

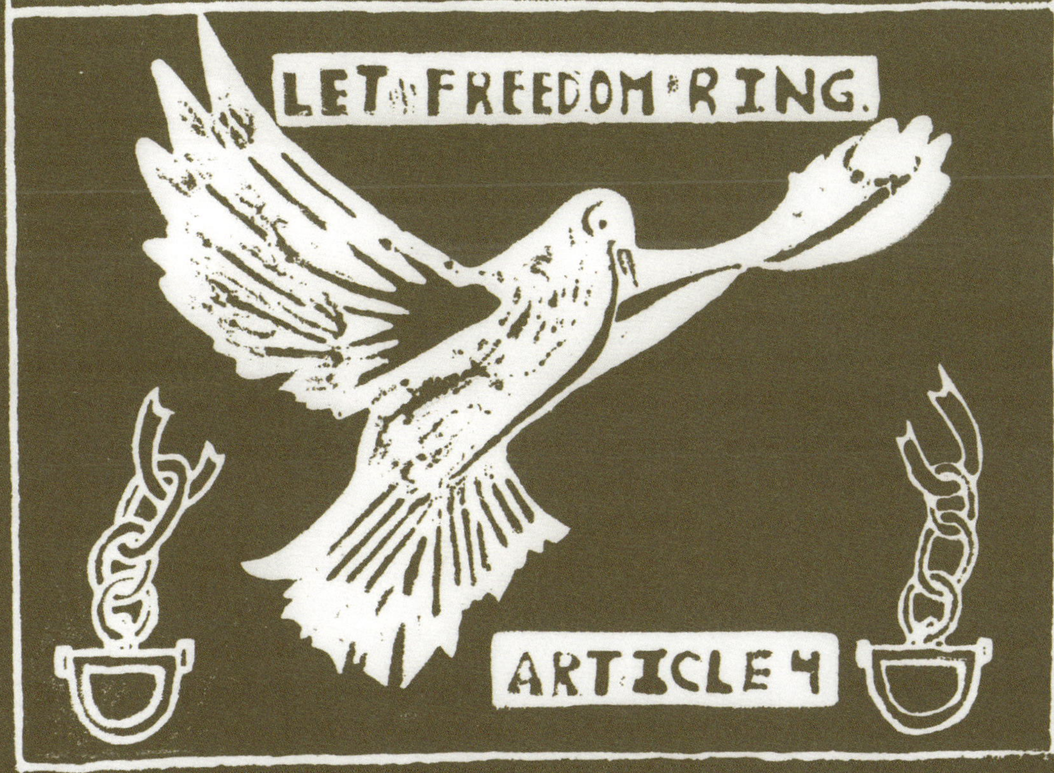

NO ONE SHALL BE HELD
IN SLAVERY OR SERVITUDE
SLAVERY AND THE SLAVE
TRADE SHALL BE PROHIBITED
IN ALL THEIR FORMS
LET FREEDOM RING.
ARTICLE 4

Article 5.

No one shall be subjected to torture or to cruel, inhuman or degrading treatment or punishment.

NO ONE SHALL BE
SUBJECTED TO TORTURE
OR TO CRUEL INHUMANE OR
DEGRADING TREATMENT
OR PUNISHMENT.
ARTICLES
DO NOT BRING BACK!

Article 6.

Everyone has the right to recognition everywhere as a person before the law.

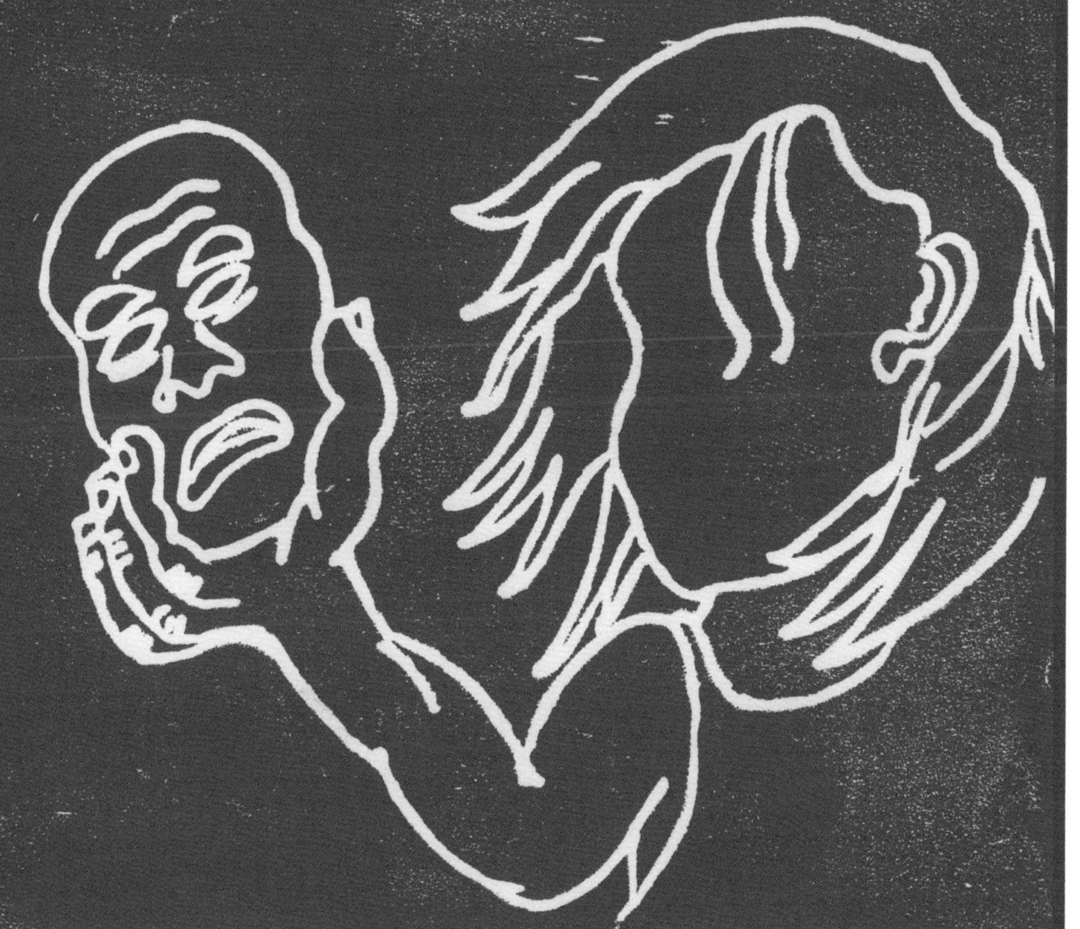

EVERYONE HAS THE RIGHT TO RECOGNITION EVERYWHERE AS A PERSON BEFORE THE LAW

Article 7.

All are equal before the law and are entitled without any discrimination to equal protection of the law. All are entitled to equal protection against any discrimination in violation of this Declaration and against any incitement to such discrimination.

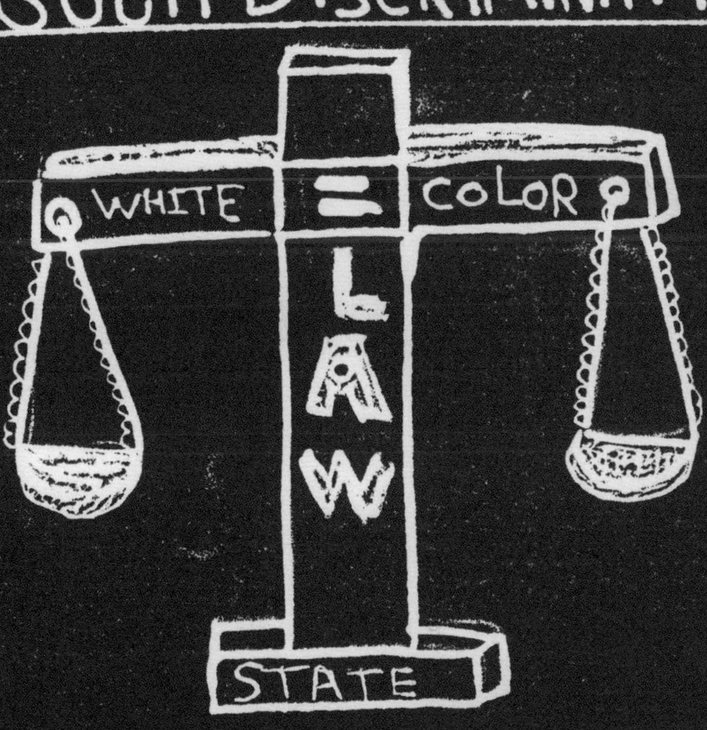
ALL ARE EQUAL BEFORE
The LAW and ARE ENTITLED WITHOUT
ANY DISCRIMINATION to EQUAL
PROTECTION of THE LAW. ALL ARE ENTITLED to
EQUAL PROTECTION AGAINST ANY
DISCRIMINATION in VIOLATION of THIS
DECLARATION and AGAINST any INCITEMENT
TO SUCH DISCRIMINATION
WHITE
=
COLOR
L
A
W
STATE

Article 8.

Everyone has the right to an effective remedy by the competent national tribunals for acts violating the fundamental rights granted him by the constitution or by law.

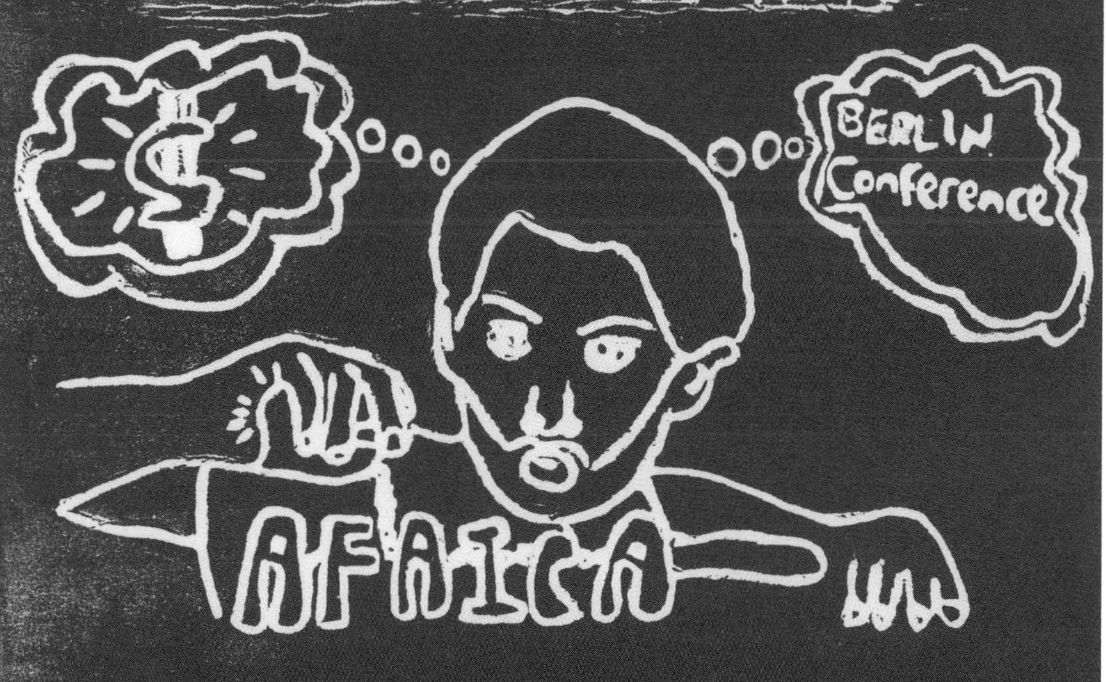

EVERYONE HAS THE RIGHT
TO AN EFFECTIVE REMEDY BY THE COMPETENT
NATIONAL TRIBUNALS FOR ACTS
VIOLATING THE FUNDAMENTAL
RIGHTS GRANTED THEM BY THE
CONSTITUTION OR BY THE LAW
ARTICLE 8
UNIVERSAL DECLARATION
OF HUMAN RIGHTS
$
BERLIN Conference
AFRICA

Article 9.

No one shall be subjected to arbitrary arrest, detention or exile.

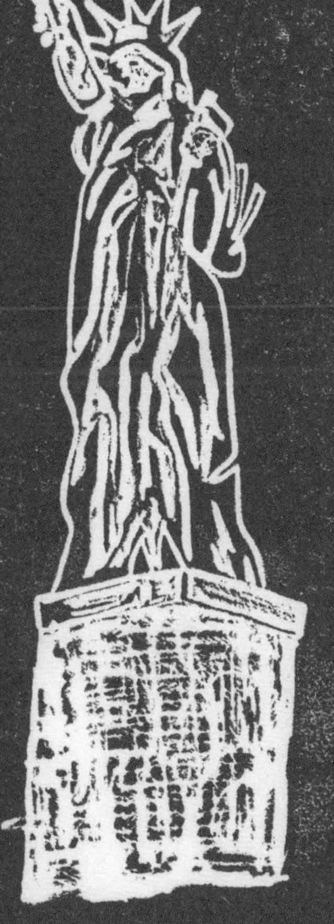

NO ONE SHALL BE
SUBJECTED TO ARBITRARY
ARREST DETENTION OR EXILE
FREEDOM

Article 10.

Everyone is entitled in full equality to a fair and public hearing by an independent and impartial tribunal, in the determination of his rights and obligations and of any criminal charge against him.

ARTICLE X

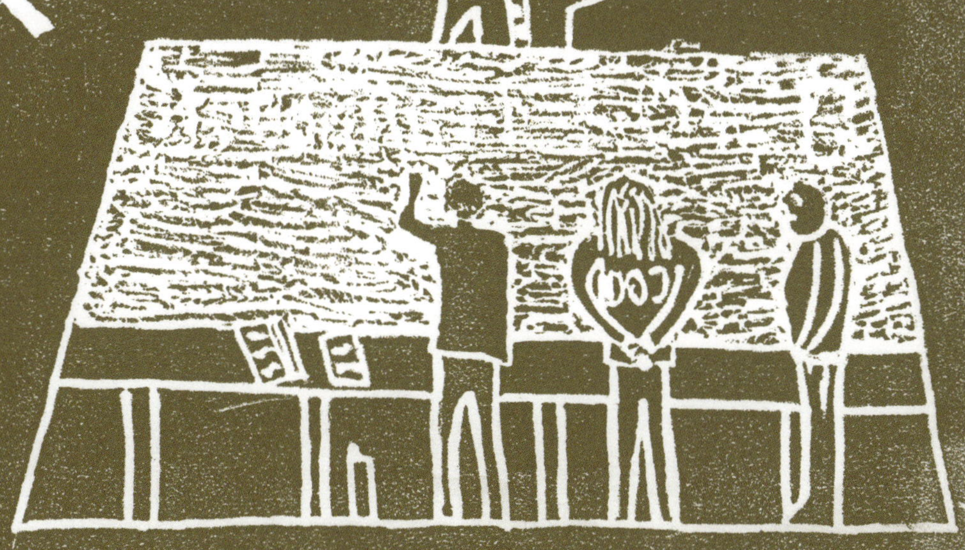

EVERYONE IS ENTITLED IN FULL EQUALITY TO A FAIR AND PUBLIC HEARING BY AN INDEPENDENT AND IMPARTIAL TRIBUNAL, IN THE DETERMINATION OF HIS (OR HER) RIGHTS AND OBLIGATIONS AND OF ANY CRIMINAL CHARGE AGAINST HIM (OR HER)

Article 11.

1. Everyone charged with a penal offence has the right to be presumed
    innocent until proved guilty according to law in a public trial at which
    he has had all the guarantees necessary for his defence.

2. No one shall be held guilty of any penal offence on account of any act
    or omission which did not constitute a penal offence, under national
    or international law, at the time when it was committed. Nor shall
    a heavier penalty be imposed than the one that was applicable at
    the time the penal offence was committed.

1 EVERYONE CHARGED WITH A PENAL OFFENCE HAS THE RIGHT TO BE PRESUMED INNOCENT UNTIL PROVED GUILTY ACCORDING TO LAW IN A PUBLIC TRIAL AT WHICH THEY HAVE HAD ALL THE GUARANTEES NECESSARY FOR THEIR DEFENCE. 2 NO ONE SHALL BE HELD GUILTY OF ANY PENAL OFFENCE ON ACCOUNT OF ANY ACT OR OMISSION WHICH DID NOT CONSTITUTE A PENAL OFFENCE, UNDER NATIONAL OR INTERNATIONAL LAW, AT THE TIME WHEN IT WAS COMMITTED. NOR SHALL A HEAVIER PENALTY BE IMPOSED THAN THE ONE THAT WAS APPLICABLE AT THE TIME THE PENAL OFFENCE WAS COMMITTED.

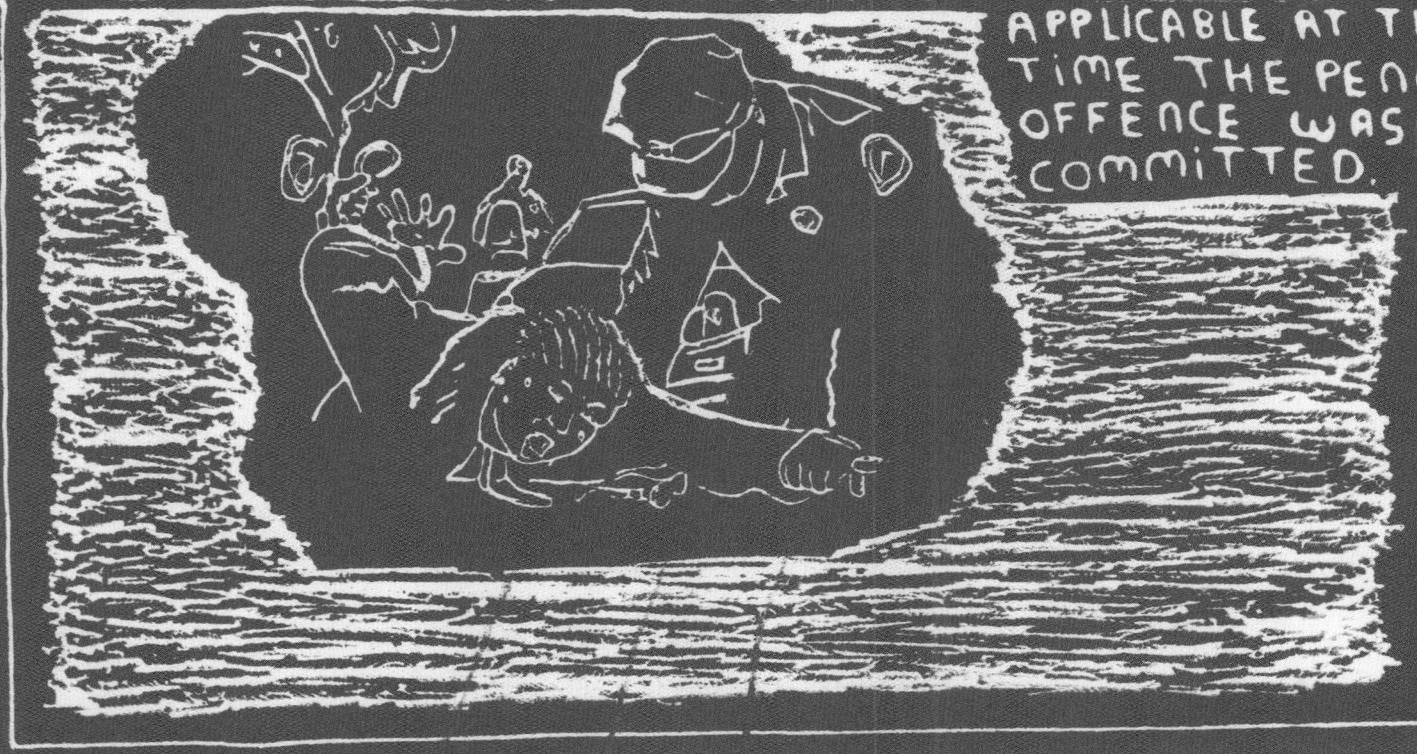

Article 12.

No one shall be subjected to arbitrary interference with his privacy, family, home or correspondence, nor to attacks upon his honour and reputation. Everyone has the right to the protection of the law against such interference or attacks.

NO ONE SHALL BE SUBJECTED
TO ARBITRARY INTERFERENCE WITH THEIR
PRIVACY, FAMILY, HOME, OR CORRESPONDENCE,
NOR TO ATTACKS UPON THEIR HONOR AND REPUTATION
EVERYONE HAS THE RIGHT TO THE PROTECTION OF THE
LAW AGAINST SUCH INTERFERENCE OR ATTACKS.
YOUR PRIVACY IS OUR OWN

Article 13.

1. Everyone has the right to freedom of movement and residence within the borders of each state.

2. Everyone has the right to leave any country, including his own, and to return to his country.

EVERYONE HAS THE RIGHT TO FREEDOM OF MOVEMENT AND RESIDENCE WITHIN THE BORDERS OF EACH STATE. EVERYONE HAS THE RIGHT TO LEAVE ANY COUNTRY INCLUDING THEIR OWN AND RETURN TO THEIR OWN COUNTRY
NONE ARE ALLOWED
WELCOME TO THE U.S.A.
NO ONE SHALL LEAVE

Article 14.

1. Everyone has the right to seek and to enjoy in other countries asylum from persecution.

2. This right may not be invoked in the case of prosecutions genuinely arising from non-political crimes or from acts contrary to the purposes and principles of the United Nations.

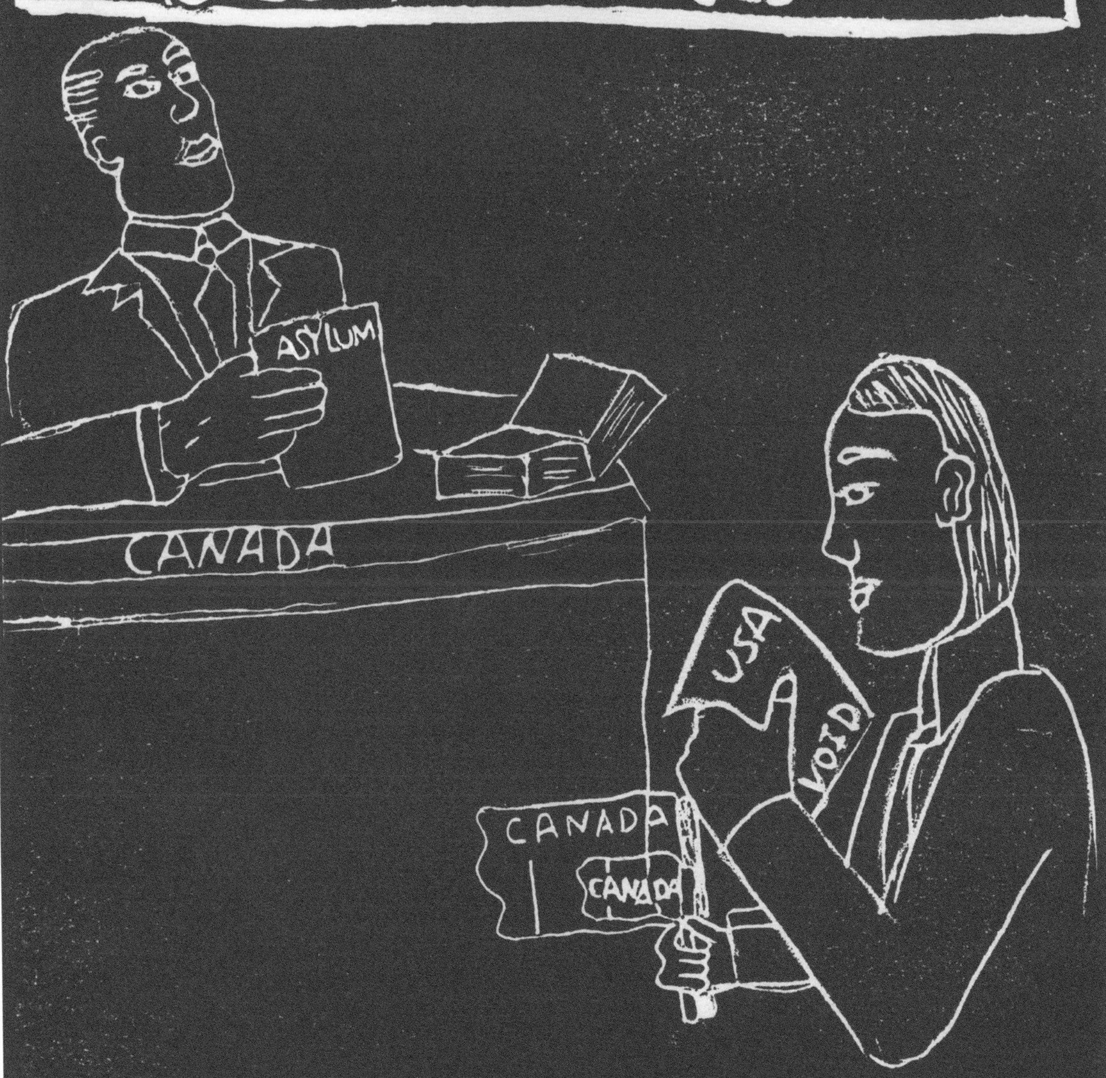

EVERYONE HAS THE RIGHT
TO SEEK AND ENJOY
IN OTHER COUNTRIES
ASYLUM FROM PERSECUTION
ASYLUM
CANADA
USA
VOID
CANADA
CANADA

Article 15.

1. Everyone has the right to a nationality.

2. No one shall be arbitrarily deprived of his nationality nor denied the right to change his nationality.

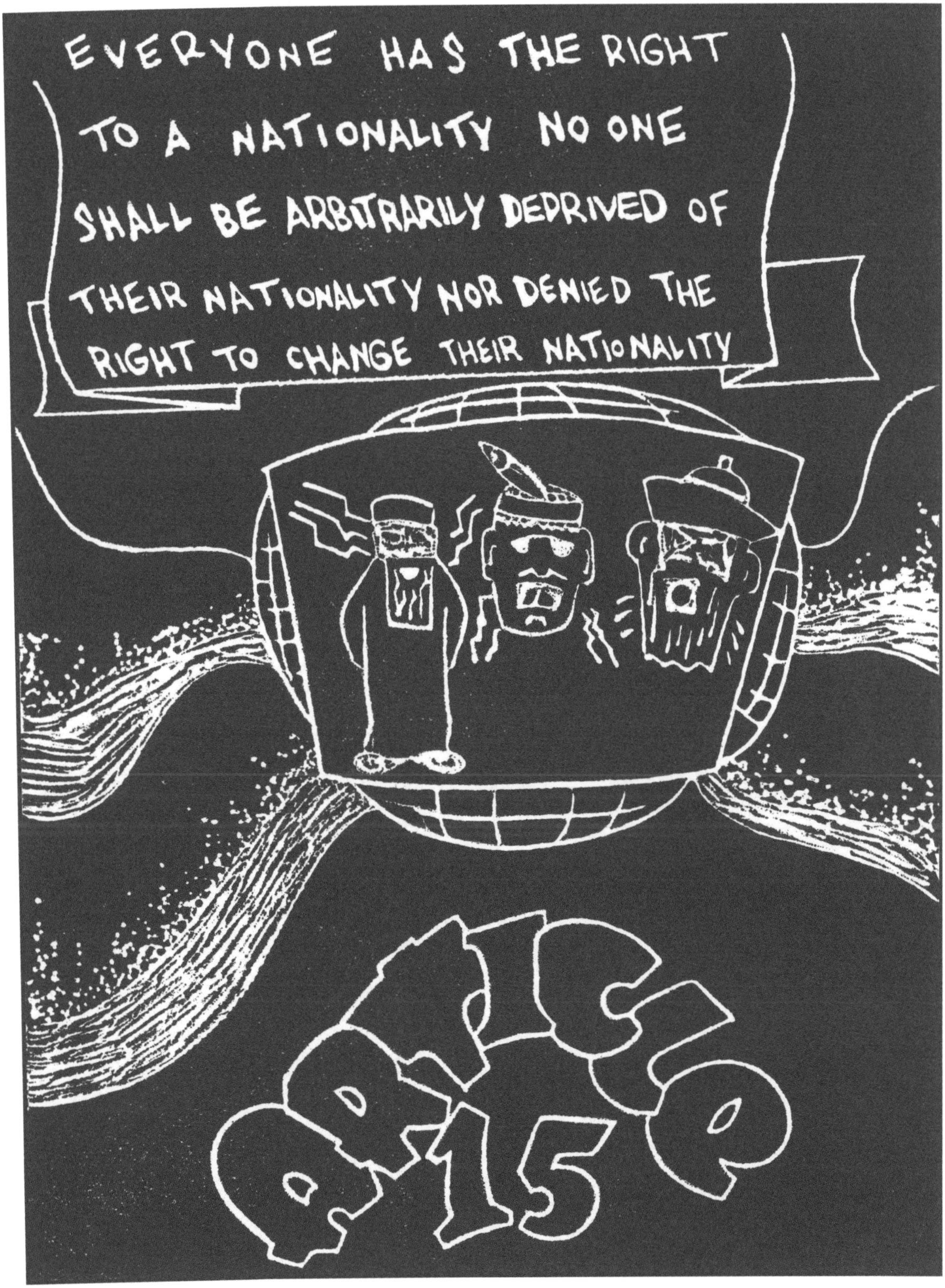

EVERYONE HAS THE RIGHT TO A NATIONALITY NO ONE SHALL BE ARBITRARILY DEDRIVED OF THEIR NATIONALITY NOR DENIED THE RIGHT TO CHANGE THEIR NATIONALITY
ARTICLE 15

Article 16.

1. Men and women of full age, without any limitation due to race, nationality or religion, have the right to marry and to found a family. They are entitled to equal rights as to marriage, during marriage and at its dissolution.

2. Marriage shall be entered into only with the free and full consent of the intending spouses.

3. The family is the natural and fundamental group unit of society and is entitled to protection by society and the State.

1. MEN AND WOMEN OF FULL AGE WITHOUT ANY limitATion DUE TO RACE NATIONALITY OR RELIGION HAVE THE RIGHT TO MARRY AND FOUND A FAMILY. THEY ARE ENTITLED TO EQUAL RIGHTS AS TO MARRIAGE AND ITS dissolUTION

2. MARRIAGE SHALL BE ENTERED INTO ONLY WITH THE FREE AND FULL CONCENT OF INTENDING SPOUSES.

3. THE FAMILY IS THE NATURAL AND FUNDAMENTAL GROUP UINT OF SOCIETY AND IS ENTITLED TO PROTECTION BY SOCIETY AND THE STATE.

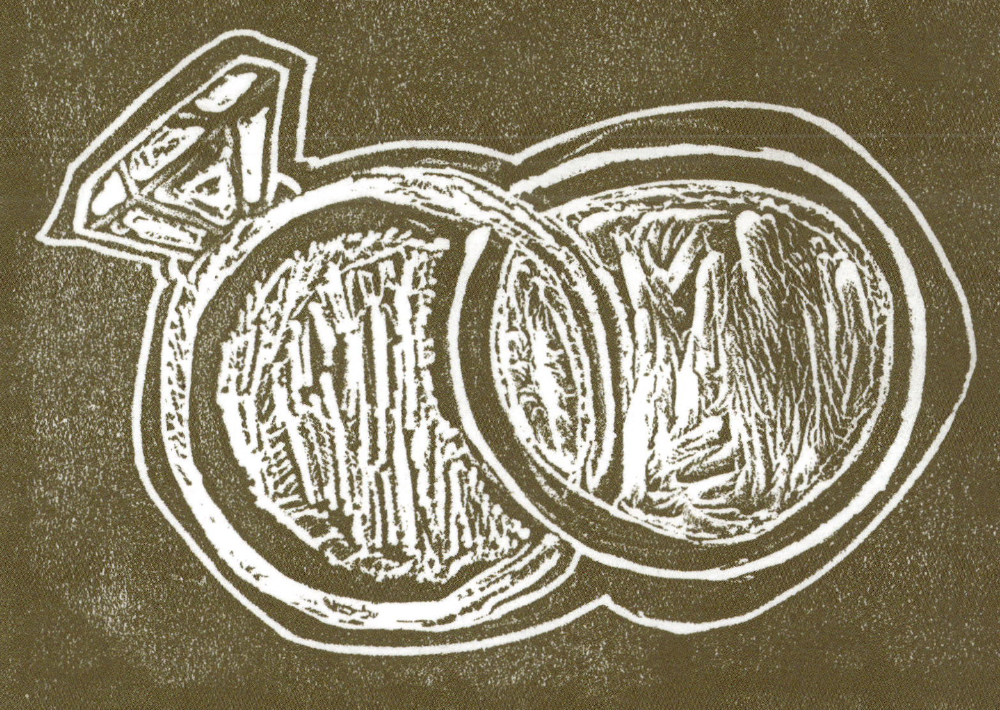

Article 17.

1. Everyone has the right to own property alone as well as in association with others.

2. No one shall be arbitrarily deprived of his property.

1 EVERYONE HAS THE RIGHT TO OWN PROPERTY
ALONE AS WELL AS IN ASSOCIATION WITH OTHERS
2 NO ONE SHALL BE ARBITRARILY DEPRIVED OF THEIR PROPERTY
ARTICLE 17

Article 18.

Everyone has the right to freedom of thought, conscience and religion; this right includes freedom to change his religion or belief, and freedom, either alone or in community with others and in public or private, to manifest his religion or belief in teaching, practice, worship and observance.

Everyone has the right to freedom of thought conscience and religion. This right includes Freedom to change their religion or belief and freedom either alone or in community with others and in public or private, to manifest their religion or belief in teaching, practice worship and observance.

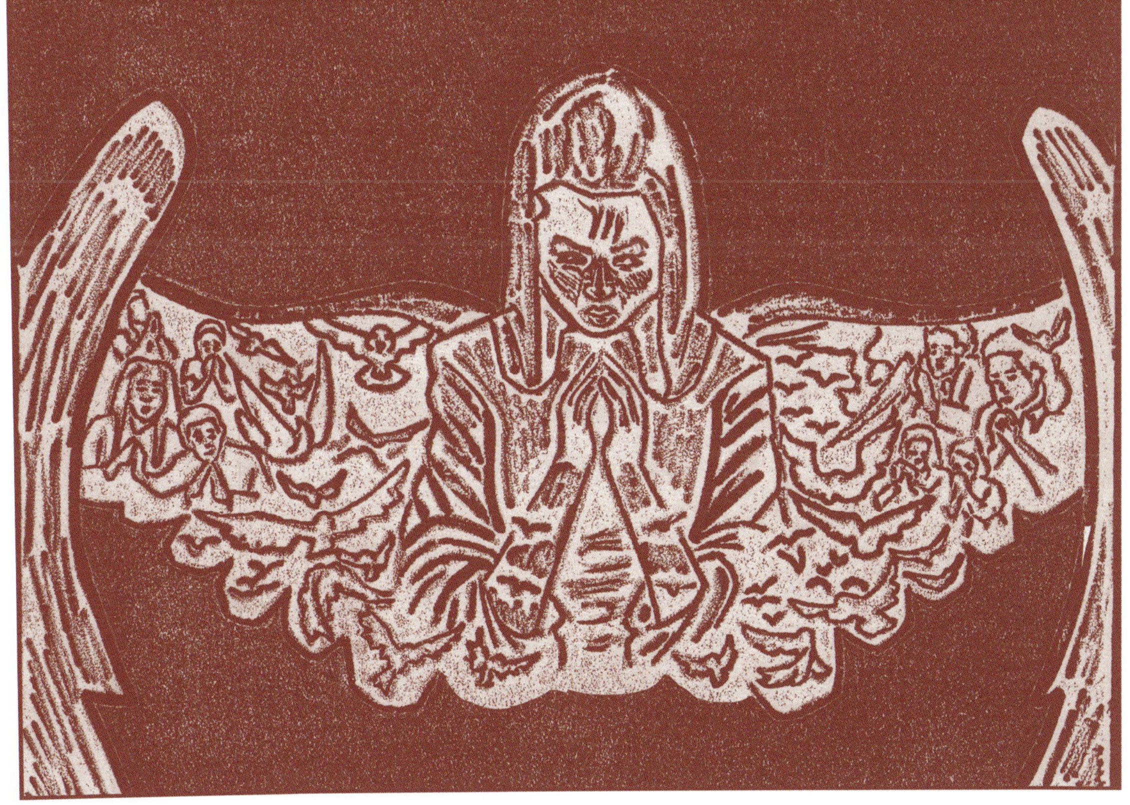

Article 19.

Everyone has the right to freedom of opinion and expression; this right includes freedom to hold opinions without interference and to seek, receive and impart information and ideas through any media and regardless of frontiers.

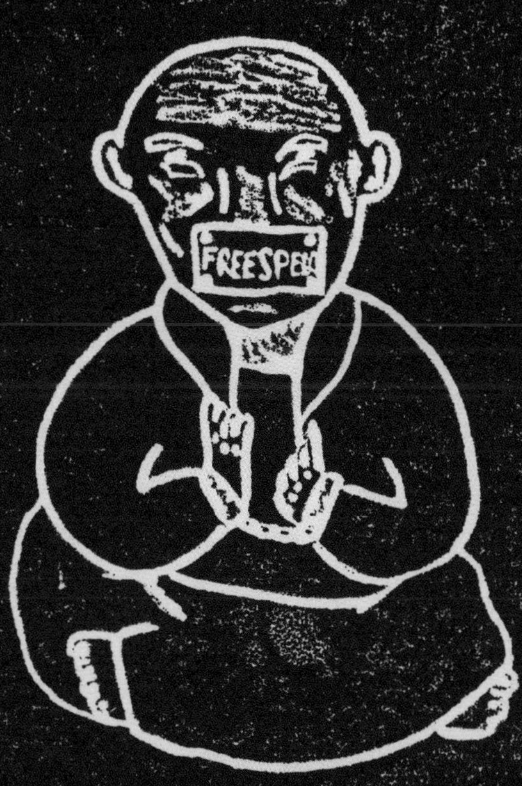

EVERYONE HAS THE RIGHT TO FREEDOM OF OPINION AND EXPRESSION THIS RIGHT INCLUDES FREEDOM TO HOLD OPINIONS WITHOUT INTERFERENCE AND TO SEEK RECEIVE AND IMPART INFORMATION AND IDEAS THROUGH ANY MEDIA AND REGARDLESS OF FRONTIERS
FREESPE

Article 20.

1. Everyone has the right to freedom of peaceful assembly and association.

2. No one may be compelled to belong to an association.

Everyone Has The Right To Freedom Of Peaceful Assembly And Association NO ONE MAY BE COMPELLED to Belong to an association

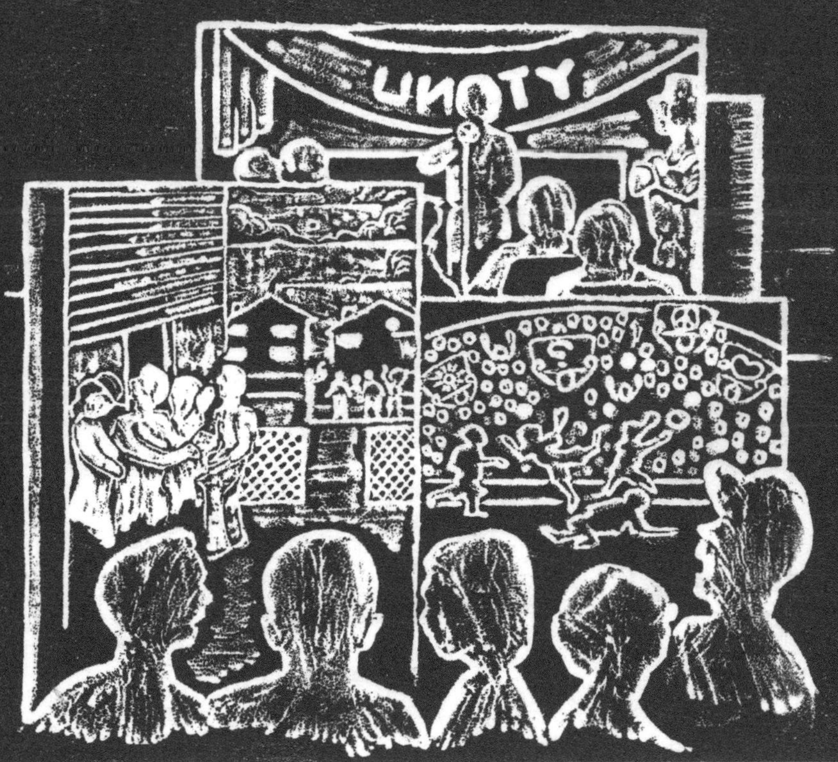

Article 21.

1. Everyone has the right to take part in the government of his country, directly or through freely chosen representatives.

2. Everyone has the right of equal access to public service in his country.

3. The will of the people shall be the basis of the authority of government; this will shall be expressed in periodic and genuine elections which shall be by universal and equal suffrage and shall be held by secret vote or by equivalent free voting procedures.

EVERYONE HAS THE RIGHT TO TAKE PART IN THE GOVERNMENT OF THEIR COUNTRY, DIRECTLY OR THROUGH FREELY CHOSEN REPRESENTATIVES. EVERYONE HAS THE RIGHT OF <u>EQUAL ACCESS</u> TO PUBLIC SERVICE IN THEIR COUNTRY. THE WILL OF THE PEOPLE SHALL BE THE BASIS OF THE AUTHORITY OF GOVERNMENT; THIS WILL SHALL BE EXPRESSED IN PERIODIC AND GENUINE ELECTIONS WHICH SHALL BE BY UNIVERSAL AND EQUAL SUFFRAGE AND SHALL BE HELD BY SECRET VOTE OR BY EQUIVALENT FREE VOTING PROCEDURES.

ARTICLE 21

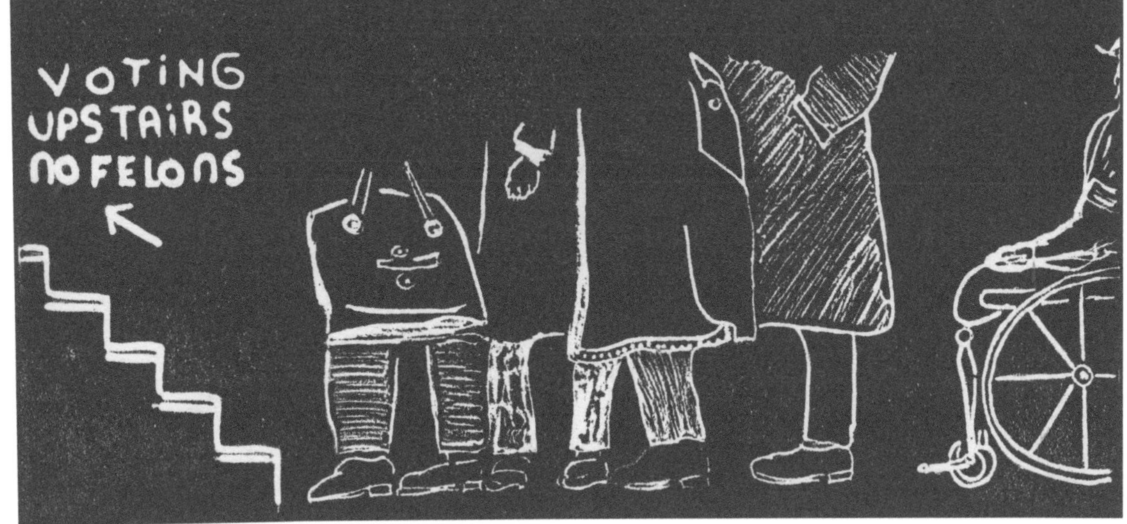

Article 22.

Everyone, as a member of society, has the right to social security and is entitled to realization, through national effort and international co-operation and in accordance with the organization and resources of each State, of the economic, social and cultural rights indispensable for his dignity and the free development of his personality.

EVERYONE AS A MEMBER OF SOCIETY HAS
THE RIGHT TO SOCIAL SECURITY AND IS
ENTITLED TO REALIZATION THROUGH
NATIONAL EFFORT AND INTERNATIONAL
CO-OPERATION AND IN ACCORDANCE WITH
THE ORGANIZATION AND RESOURCES OF
EACH STATE OF THE ECONOMIC SOCIAL
AND CULTURAL RIGHTS INDISPENSABLE
FOR HIS DIGNITY AND THE FREE
DEVELOPMENT OF HIS PERSONALITY

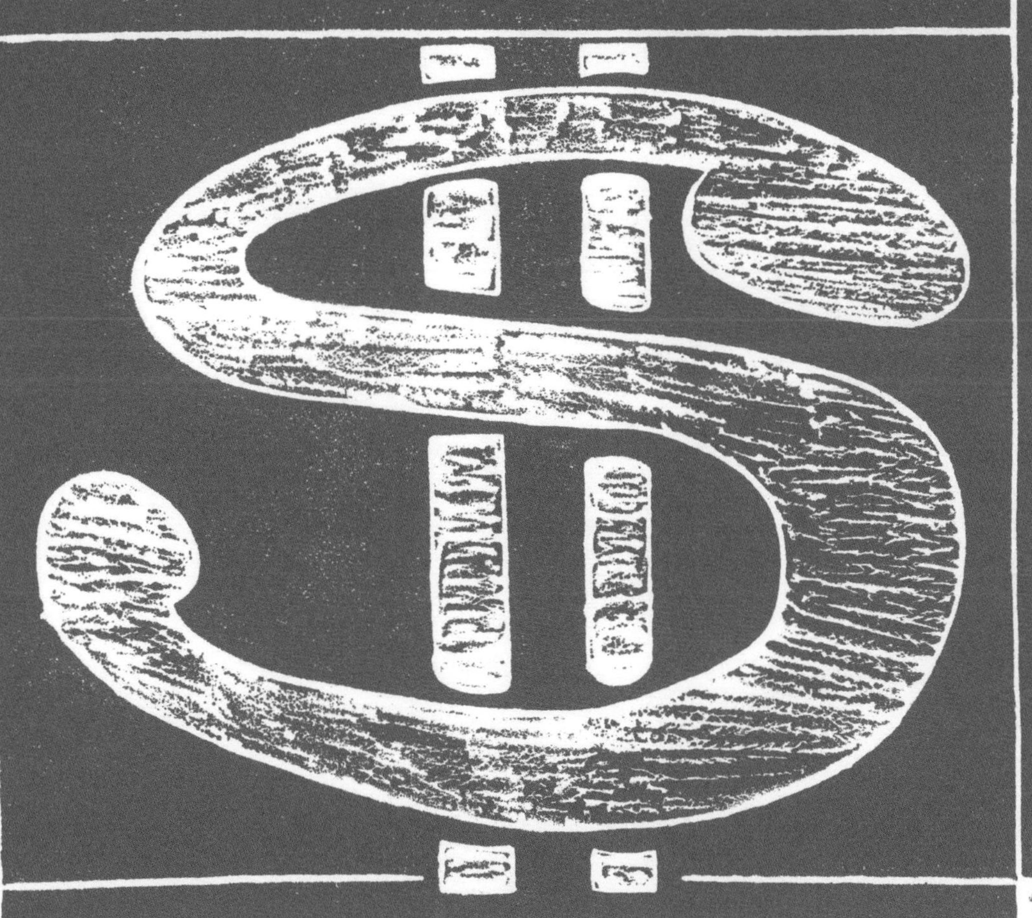

Article 23.

1. Everyone has the right to work, to free choice of employment, to just and favourable conditions of work and to protection against unemployment.

2. Everyone, without any discrimination, has the right to equal pay for equal work.

3. Everyone who works has the right to just and favourable remuneration ensuring for himself and his family an existence worthy of human dignity, and supplemented, if necessary, by other means of social protection.

4. Everyone has the right to form and to join trade unions for the protection of his interests.

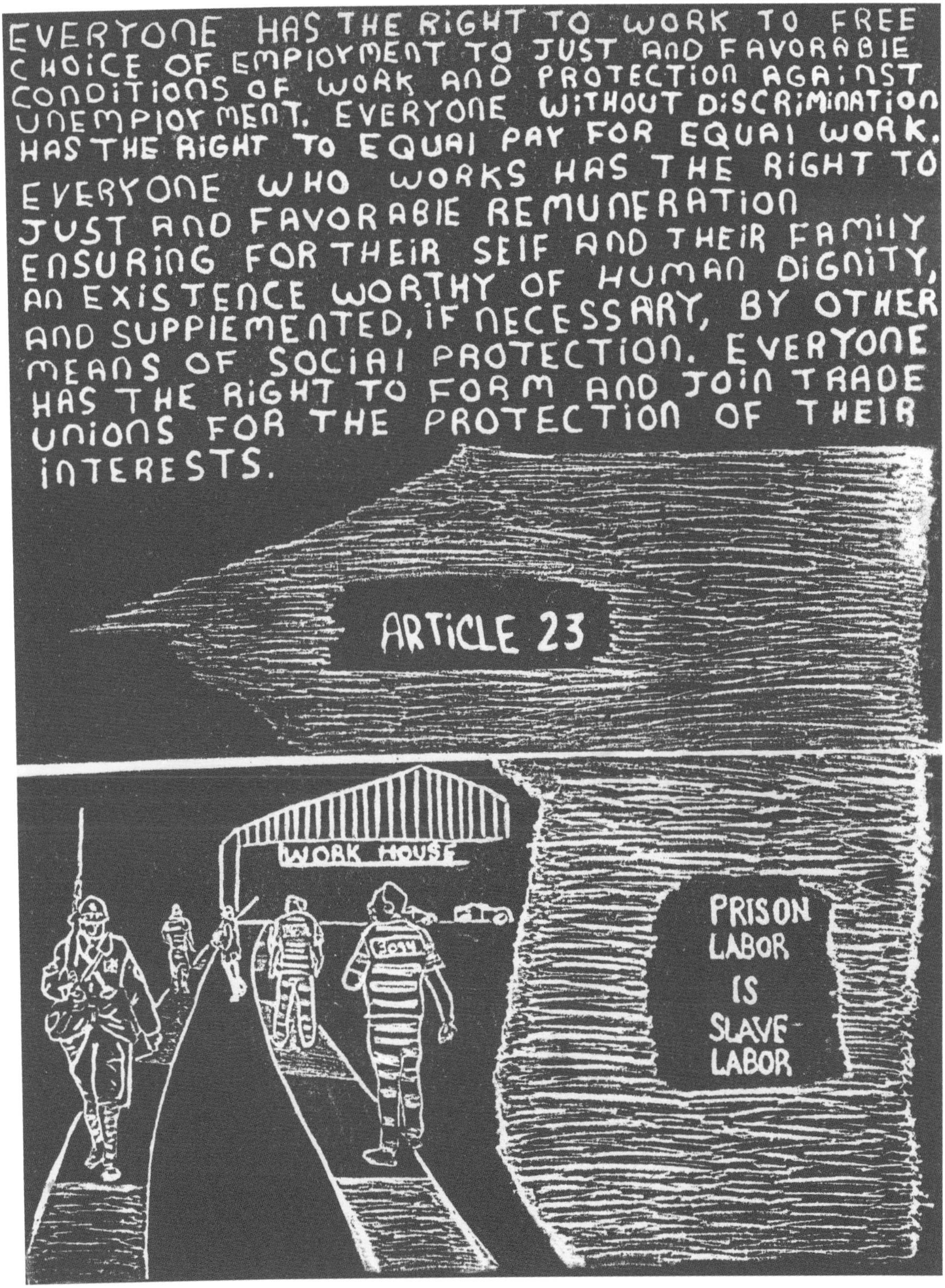

EVERYONE HAS THE RIGHT TO WORK TO FREE CHOICE OF EMPLOYMENT TO JUST AND FAVORABLE CONDITIONS OF WORK AND PROTECTION AGAINST UNEMPLOYMENT. EVERYONE WITHOUT DISCRIMINATION HAS THE RIGHT TO EQUAL PAY FOR EQUAL WORK. EVERYONE WHO WORKS HAS THE RIGHT TO JUST AND FAVORABLE REMUNERATION ENSURING FOR THEIR SELF AND THEIR FAMILY AN EXISTENCE WORTHY OF HUMAN DIGNITY, AND SUPPLEMENTED, IF NECESSARY, BY OTHER MEANS OF SOCIAL PROTECTION. EVERYONE HAS THE RIGHT TO FORM AND JOIN TRADE UNIONS FOR THE PROTECTION OF THEIR INTERESTS.
ARTICLE 23
WORK HOUSE
PRISON LABOR IS SLAVE-LABOR

Article 24.

Everyone has the right to rest and leisure, including reasonable limitation of working hours and periodic holidays with pay.

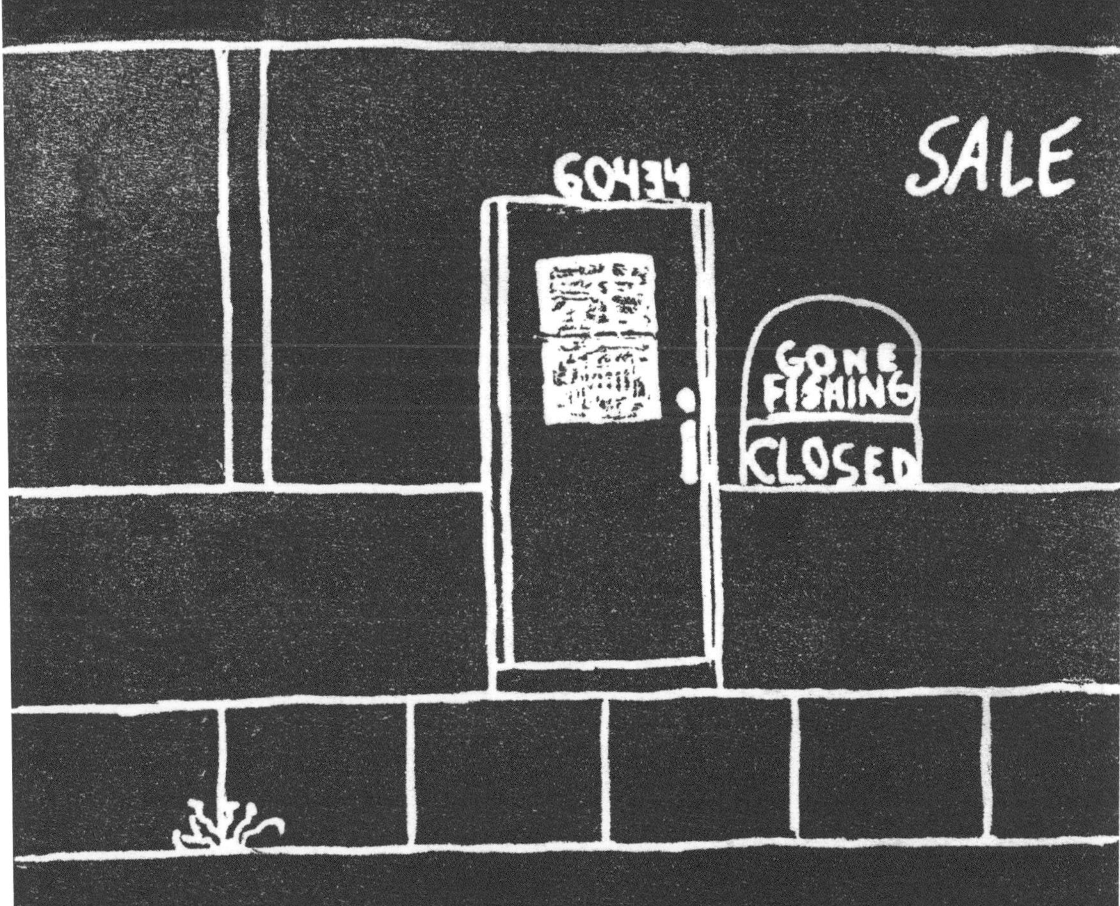

EVERYONE HAS THE RIGHT TO REST AND LEISURE INCLUDING REASONABLE LIMITATION OF WORKING HOURS AND PERIODIC HOLIDAYS WITH PAY
60434
SALE
GONE FISHING
CLOSED

Article 25.

1. Everyone has the right to a standard of living adequate for the health
    and well-being of himself and of his family, including food, clothing,
    housing and medical care and necessary social services, and the right
    to security in the event of unemployment, sickness, disability, widow-
    hood, old age or other lack of livelihood in circumstances beyond his
    control.

2. Motherhood and childhood are entitled to special care and assistance.
    All children, whether born in or out of wedlock, shall enjoy the same
    social protection.

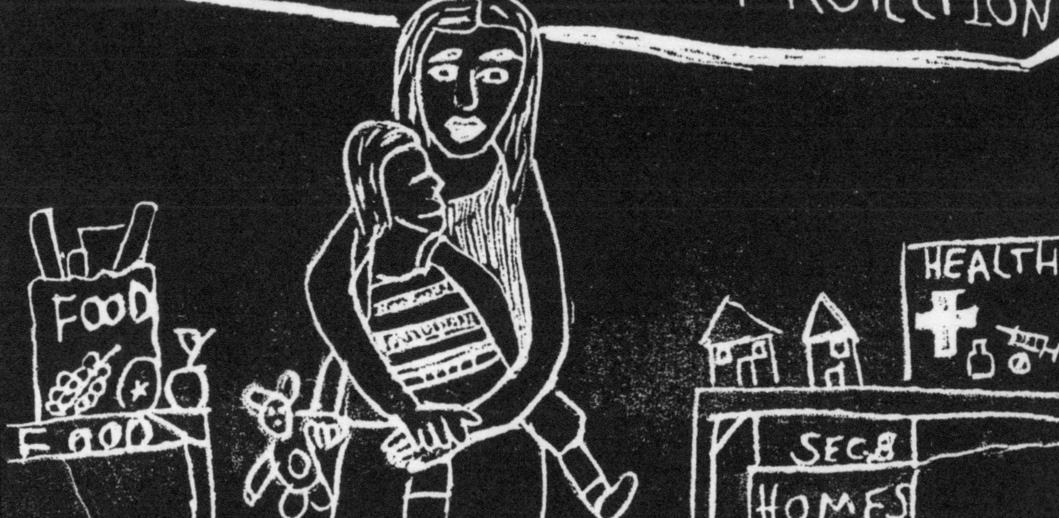

EVERYONE HAS THE RIGHT
TO A STANDARD OF LIVING ADEQUATE FOR THE HEALTH
AND WELL-BEING OF THEIR SELF AND OF THEIR
FAMILY INCLUDING FOOD CLOTHING HOUSING AND MEDICAL
CARE AND NECESSARY SOCIAL SERVICES AND THE RIGHT
TO SECURITY IN THE EVENT OF UNEMPLOYMENT SICKNESS
DISABILITY .WIDOWHOOD .OLD AGE OR OTHER LACK OF
LIVELIHOOD IN CIRCUMSTANCESS BEYOND THEIR CONTROL
MOTHERHOOD AND CHILDHOOD ARE ENTITLED
TO SPECIAL CARE AND ASSISTANE ALL CHILDREN
WHETHER BORN IN OR OUT OF WEDLOCK SHALL ENJOY THE
SAME SOCIAL PROTECTION
FOOD
FOOD
HEALTH
SEC8
HOMES

Article 26.

1. Everyone has the right to education. Education shall be free, at least
    in the elementary and fundamental stages. Elementary education shall
    be compulsory. Technical and professional education shall be made
    generally available and higher education shall be equally accessible
    to all on the basis of merit.

2. Education shall be directed to the full development of the human
    personality and to the strengthening of respect for human rights
    and fundamental freedoms. It shall promote understanding, tolerance
    and friendship among all nations, racial or religious groups, and shall
    further the activities of the United Nations for the maintenance
    of peace.

3. Parents have a prior right to choose the kind of education that shall
    be given to their children.

EVERYONE HAS THE RIGHT TO

1 EDUCATION, EDUCATION SHALL BE FREE, AT LEAST IN THE ELEMENTARY AND FUNDAMENTAL STAGES. ELEMENTARY EDUCATION SHALL BE COMPULSORY. TECHNICAL AND PROFESSIONAL EDUCATION SHALL BE MADE GENERALLY AVAILABLE AND HIGHER EDUCATION SHALL BE EQUALLY ACCESSIBLE TO ALL ON THE BASIS OF MERIT. 2 EDUCATION SHALL BE DIRECTED TO THE FULL DEVELOPMENT OF THE HUMAN PERSONALITY AND TO THE STRENGTHENING OF RESPECT FOR HUMAN RIGHTS AND FUNDAMENTAL FREEDOMS. IT SHALL PROMOTE UNDERSTANDING. TOLERANCE AND FRIENDSHIP AMONG ALL NATIONS. 'RACAIL' OR RELIGIOUS GROUPS, AND SHALL FURTHER THE ACTIVITIES OF THE UNITED NATIONS FOR THE MAINTENANCE OF PEACE 3 PARENTS HAVE A PRIOR RIGHT TO CHOOSE THE KIND OF EDUCATION THAT SHALL BE GIVEN TO THEIR CHILDREN.

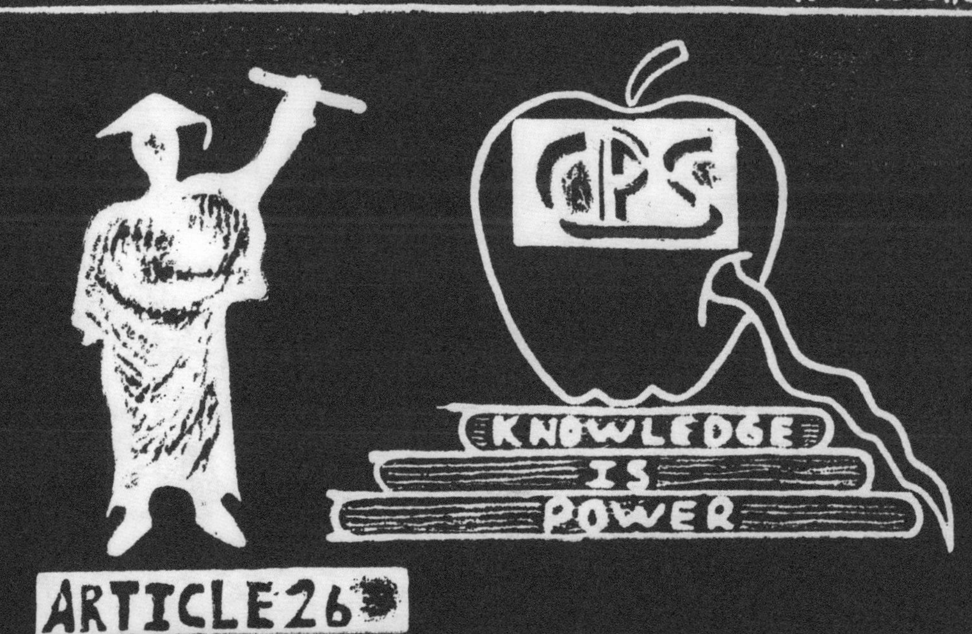

Article 27.

1. Everyone has the right freely to participate in the cultural life of the community, to enjoy the arts and to share in scientific advancement and its benefits.

2. Everyone has the right to the protection of the moral and material interests resulting from any scientific, literary or artistic production of which he is the author.

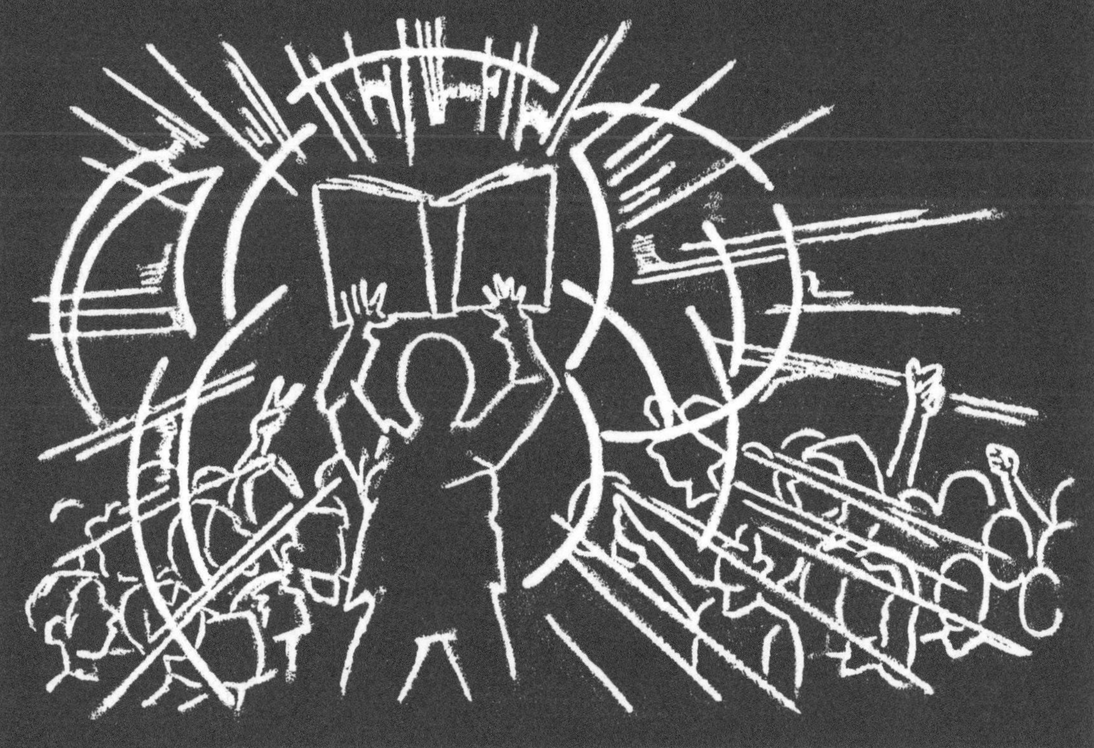

Everyone has the right freely to participate in the cultural life of the community, to enjoy the arts and to share in scientific advancement and its benefits.
EVERYONE has the right...!
...to the protection of the moral and material interests resulting from any scientific, literary or artistic production of which they are the author.

Article 28.

Everyone is entitled to a social and international order in which the rights and freedoms set forth in this Declaration can be fully realized.

EVRYONE IS **ENTITLED** TO SOCIAL AND INTERNATIONAL ORDER IN WHICH THE RIGHT AND FREEDOMS SET FORTH IN THIS DECLARATION CAN BE FULLY REALIZED BELIEVE, SUPPORT, AND PROTECT SEXUAL ASSAULT SURVIVORS

IN THE US RAPE is NORMALIZED EXCUSED THIS ENVIRONMENT DISSUADES PEOPLE FROM REPORTING ASSAULT AND MAKES IT NEARLY IMPOSSBIE FOR SURVIVORS TO OBTAIN JUSTICE IN MILITARY OR CIVLIAN COUR SYSTEMS

HELPLINE

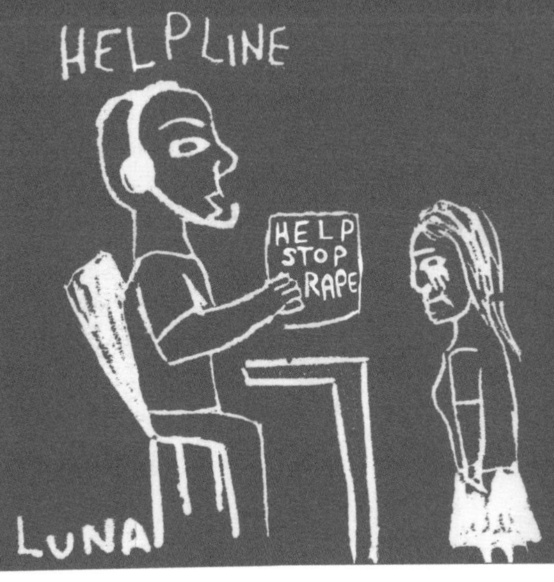

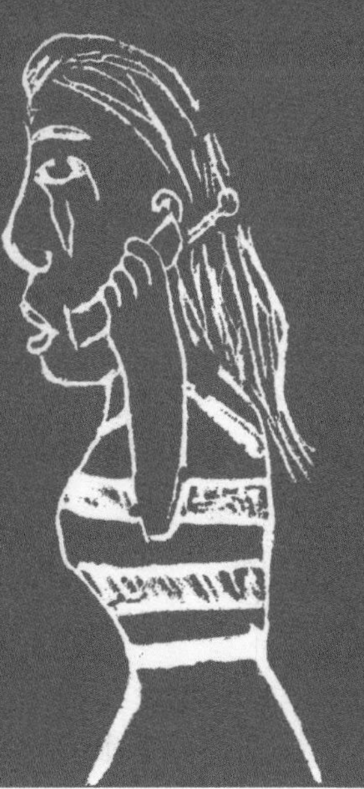

Article 29.

1.   Everyone has duties to the community in which alone the free and full development of his personality is possible.

2.   In the exercise of his rights and freedoms, everyone shall be subject only to such limitations as are determined by law solely for the purpose of securing due recognition and respect for the rights and freedoms of others and of meeting the just requirements of morality, public order and the general welfare in a democratic society.

3.   These rights and freedoms may in no case be exercised contrary to the purposes and principles of the United Nations.

1. EVERYONE HAS DUTIES
TO THE COMMUNITY IN WHICH ALONE THE FREE AND FULL
DEVELOPMENT OF THEIR PERSONALITY IS POSSIBLE
2 IN THE EXERCISE OF THEIR RIGHTS AND FREEDOMS,
EVERYONE SHALL BE SUBJECT ONLY TO SUCH LIMITATIONS AS
ARE DETERMIND BY LAW SOLELY FOR THE PURPOSE OF SECURING
DUE RECOGNITION AND RESPECT FOR THE RIGHTS AND FREEDOMS
OF OTHERS AND OF MEETING THE JUST REQUIREMENTS OF MORALITY
PUBLIC ORDER AND THE GENERAL WELFARE IN A DEMOCRATIC
SOCIETY 3 THESE RIGHTS AND FREEDOMS MAY IN NO CASE
BE EXERCISED CONTRARY TO THE PURPOSES AND
PRINCIPLES OF THE UNITED NATIONS.
FREEDOM
ARTICLE 29

Article 30.

Nothing in this Declaration may be interpreted as implying for any State, group or person any right to engage in any activity or to perform any act aimed at the destruction of any of the rights and freedoms set forth herein.

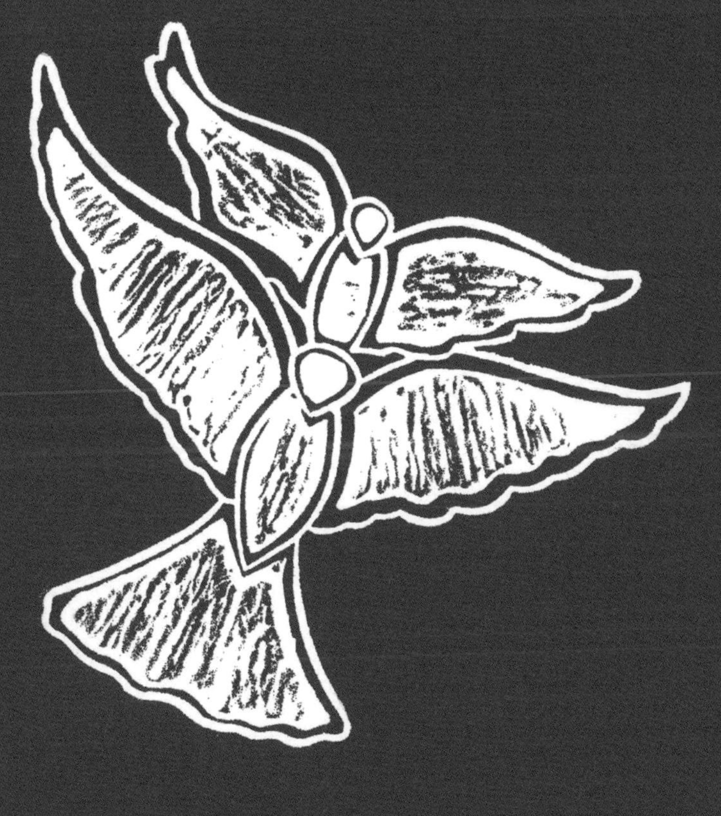

NOTHING IN THIS DECLARATION
MAY BE INTERPRETED AS IMPLYING
FOR ANY STATE GROUP OR PERSON
ANY RIGHT TO ENGAGE IN ANY
ACTIVITY OR TO PERFORM ANY ACT
AIMED AT THE DESTRUCTION OF ANY
THE RIGHTS AND FREEDOMS
SET FORTH HEREIN

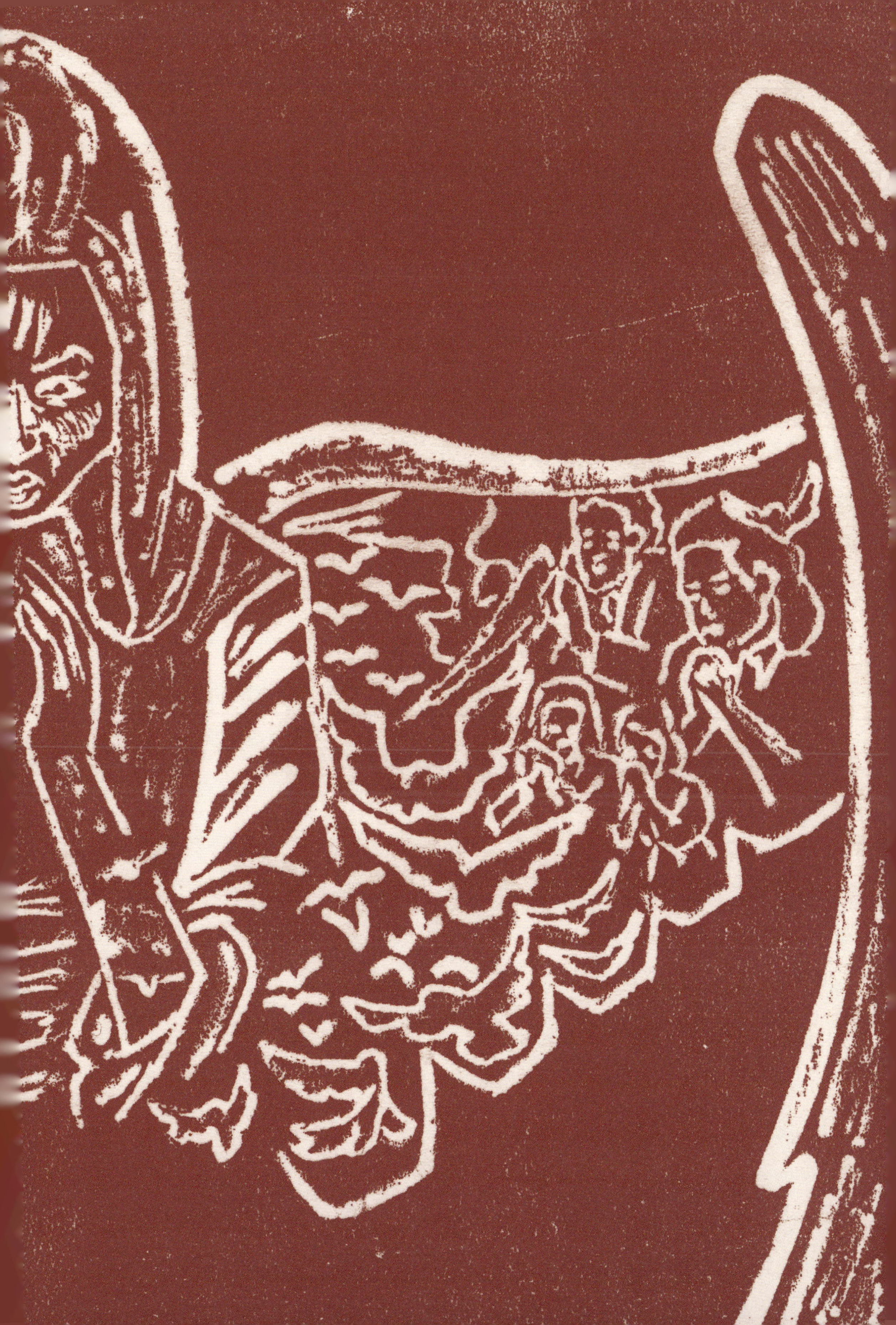

Barbara Ransby

REFLECTIONS ON TEACHING AT STATEVILLE PRISON

« Charles McLaurin, *UDHR Article 18* (Detail), 2018

Most Americans have not been inside a U.S. prison. I would venture to guess, however, based on the demographics of targeted mass incarceration, most Black Americans have, either as a visitor or as an incarcerated person. Everyone should visit a prison at least once. It will make the call for prison abolition and universal inalienable rights much easier to understand.

As a part of the Prison + Neighborhood Arts/Education Program (P+NAP), I have had the privilege to teach and to lecture briefly at Illinois' Stateville Prison, a maximum-security men's prison outside Chicago. My students were smart, insightful, engaged, and as is sometimes the case, they may have taught me as much or more than I taught them. We talked about the U.S. Civil Rights and Black Power movements, Ella Baker, and the Movement for Black Lives. We also talked about gender, sexism, and violence. I don't know what my students' crimes were, but through their comments in class, I gleaned that most of them had done some pretty heinous things. They had regrets, remorse, and sober reflections on their lives before Stateville. But the challenge for me was could I see them as "just students?" Could I see beyond the harm they had caused, the violent acts they may have perpetrated, the hard lives they had lived? Could we put all that aside and talk about ideas, history, theory, and art? Well, yes and no. We all brought who we were to that classroom. And if we dared to forget where we were or who they were, there were armed guards, steel bars, blue prison uniforms, and a looming obsolete gun tower just outside our small classroom to remind us. Still we formed an odd, fragile, and dynamic learning community for the weeks I was there.

I cannot fully attest to what my Stateville students learned. There were no tests or any of the usual, fraught metrics of academic achievement. I do know that they were some of the most conscientious students I have ever shared a learning space with. Most of them brought underlined copies of my book to class, had taken extensive notes in the margins, asked lots of questions, and were never shy to speak up. In all of my classes, the students were all Black with one or two Latinx students in the mix. Like any collection of people, there were different personalities. One guy sat in the corner looking skeptical and slightly annoyed from day one. But then we got onto a topic that excited him and piqued his interest and he was "all in." Another student was eager and loquacious every class session, barely leaving room for others to chime in. A third student I remember quite vividly: baby face, sad eyes, and a demeanor that seemed as sweet and gentle as any person I have ever met. I wondered what he was thinking. He nodded at the comments of others, let out a low volume "uh huh," now and then, but was otherwise quiet and politely withdrawn. One of the few comments he made was, "I don't know too much about that—I been locked up since I was 17." And then he dropped his head as if he was ashamed or embarrassed by that fact. He was in his late 20s at the time of the class.

In addition to the students' engagement with me, I noticed the interactions they had with one another, which in contrast to the television version of prison antagonisms, grudges, and hostilities, there was amazing camaraderie among my students. One day, a talkative student was uncharacteristically quiet. "What's up?" I asked. Another student intervened. "He's just dealing with some stuff right now. He'll be alright." I never knew what "stuff" my student was dealing with, but his friend did. Maybe there was a fight in the yard. Maybe he had somehow missed a visit from his children or had gotten bad news from home. There was an evident support system that existed even in the confining and emotionally debilitating prison environment. In other exchanges there was genuine collegiality. Students affirmed one another's comments about the readings, disagreed respectfully, referenced one another's earlier insights, and apologized for interrupting or jumping the queue. They were not angels or perfect people by any stretch. But they seemingly valued their special time together on Fridays at 1:00 p.m. when they were not their Department of Corrections assigned number but were treated, and able to treat each other, as discussants, debaters, knowledge seekers, philosophers, fellow students, and, if only for a carved out chunk of time, full-fledged autonomous human beings.

Entering Stateville every week I was painfully aware that our semi-autonomous little classroom with the blank, paint-chipped walls and steel desks was one small oasis of calmness and freedom inside a larger institution that was the antithesis of both. Prisons exude fear, control, surveillance, precarity, and routinized humiliations. When you walk in, even though some of the prison guards themselves seem uncomfortable with the invasive procedures that are required, nevertheless, they play the roles they have been assigned. You walk into the grungy little waiting room filled with vending machines, families, mothers, and friends of the men on the other side. There is fear even at that stage. Will there be a routine "lock down," in which both visits and classes are cancelled? Even if a wife has taken off work, a mother has paid a neighbor to drive her there, a friend is coming to bring news of illness or death in the family, "no visitors today," means everything is shut down. You turn around and go home and try another day. Before you even arrive, you are given a list of things you cannot wear: sleeveless dresses and blouses, low cut tops, skirts above the knee, sports bras. After that hurdle, then there is the search. After showing identification and waiting, one is buzzed into the search room. Take off your shoes and show the bottoms. Lift your bra. Raise your arms to be thoroughly patted down. We then walk across a stark open field to another building where papers are searched, books are leafed through, more questions are asked until finally bars slide open and we walk down a long dim corridor, out another set of doors and across another field to the "education building." And yes, another set of questions from a guard sitting at a little desk at the entrance. Finally, we are ushered into our classrooms and the students file in.

The first day of class I greet each of my 15 students with a personal introduction and handshake. I wanted to connect with them. I wanted to show respect and warmth. I wanted to build a little bit of trust. But on day one, I have to admit, I was also a little bit afraid. These were tough guys. I was a middle-aged college professor living a fairly comfortable life far away from Stateville. Would they resent me coming in to create these artificial two hours of normalcy and fleeing back to the comforts of my own life? Would they try to mock or manipulate me? Would they try to intimidate me? My own biases and ignorance had informed those fears. They were indeed tough guys, but they were so much more complicated and interesting than that.

Even though my Stateville students were diverse in age, personality, and views, there were some things they shared in common, which is important to remember when we advocate for the abolition of prisons based on human rights. These common experiences came out in the course of classroom discussions about race, power, gender, and economic justice. They grew up poor. They had been poorly educated and/or pushed out of public schools early in life. They had trouble finding or keeping good-paying jobs. They had been witnesses to or victims of violence, including by school security guards and police. A surprising number had witnessed domestic violence as children.

I learned a lot from my students at Stateville. I was reminded that we are all multi-faceted human creatures, and none of us are defined by any single thing we do. All of us change and evolve. There are not good people and bad people but good and bad actions we are all capable of. We are works in progress. And prisons—cramped, rigid, warehouses filled with cages and caged ambitions—neither keep the rest of us safe, nor encourage the growth and betterment of those inside. The people that are held there manage to grow and evolve despite the prison environment, not because of it. As Angela Davis suggests in the title of her landmark book on the subject, we need to build a society in which prisons are indeed, "obsolete." Their continued existence diminishes us all.

For me, and many others, however, the call for the abolition of prisons is not a single demand, or a single issue. It is wrapped up in the struggle for truly universal rights and a myriad of systemic changes that need to occur in tandem with the dismantling of prisons, jails, and police forces. These institutions don't exist in a political or economic vacuum. Prisons are not just warehouses for Black and Brown bodies, they are containers for poor and working-class bodies that are disproportionately people of color. There are a few rich people in jail, but not many. The Bernie Madoffs of the world don't end up there. Most of my students were in prison for crimes against property. Some of those crimes were committed with guns and during the commission of those crimes, sometimes innocent people were hurt or even killed. There is no justification for that. However, the impetus, the root cause of the crime itself was that people did not have what they needed to have a decent life, or what they felt they needed. And so, they took it, or entered into the dangerous informal economy to make a living. Imagine if we lived in a more egalitarian society where we were not measured or evaluated by the stuff we have, and everyone had what they needed to have a decent life. Then we could focus on the other big triggers for violent crimes, misogyny, mental illness, and toxic masculinity. So, conflict resolution strategies, domestic violence prevention, mental health for all, and feminist education workshops could potentially change the behavior of men who commit acts of violence to somehow prove they are "men," as well as women who commit harm out of anger, frustration, or desperation. These interventions would reduce harm considerably. But when harm does occur, restorative justice is a model that factors in healing, acknowledges our shared humanity, and looks to making amends for hurt or damage that is caused.

So, my biggest take away from my experience at Stateville is that the call for prison abolition and human rights, which I think all my co-teachers share, has to be coupled with a call for the dismantling of racial capitalism. Capitalism promotes inequality and legitimates poverty and want. Capitalism creates ruthless competition that spills over from the boardrooms to the street with deadly consequences. With wealth increasingly concentrated in fewer and fewer hands, folks at the bottom of the economic hierarchy are essentially abandoned in terms of jobs, services, and access to life-sustaining resources. Inequality and disparity, enforced through the reality or threat of state violence, are legitimized according to the rules of capitalism. Therefore, more and more people are breaking the rules in order to survive. Violence is often the byproduct of this rule breaking. Perhaps needless to say, the irony and duplicity at play here is that so much violence is enacted, so much theft committed, and suffering caused by the policies of elite politicians and wealthy corporations; legalized harm, which is rewarded, not punished.

As a historian, most of my course content at Stateville dealt with the past, but occasionally, we drifted into discussion about contemporary issues. During one class session we landed on the topic of Black Lives Matter. "What would you say if you could speak directly to the leaders of the Black Lives Matter movement and the Movement for Black Lives?" I asked my Stateville students. "Tell them don't forget about us. Our Black lives matter too," one student said after a long period of silence. Others nodded in agreement. The Movement for Black Lives (M4BL), a coalition of over 100 groups emerging out of the "Black Lives Matter" protests of the past six to seven years has operated through an abolitionist and human rights framework. In other words, they have not forgotten the million plus incarcerated Black people in this country. Their work and the related spontaneous demonstrations, vigils, marches, and uprisings have challenged the underlying logic of prisons and of racial capitalism. To its credit, this movement has eschewed the "politics of respectability," and the prison and sentencing policies based on punishment and revenge, which essentially write off people deemed "bad" by the system. They are advocating, instead, humane, compassionate, forward-looking policies and practices that address the underlying causes of harm-inducing behavior and violence. They are doing so through campaigns like the "Free them All" and "Black Mamas Bail Out" campaigns, and in documents like "Vision for Black Lives," and "The Breathe Act." If they win, we all win. If they win, my students at Stateville get a second chance, or at least the next generation of would-be Stateville "inmates" have the potential to learn and grow and contribute and make amends for their mistakes outside of prison walls, and institutions like Stateville will be truly obsolete.

Flynard N. Miller, Freedom, 2016 »

GIVE ME

OR

GIVE M

REEDOM
E DEATH

Asylum

Means protection

As in open
Arms

Like when
Abuelita opens

Her blue bata or
Red robe—her ancient

Yellow sweater—to
Hug or hold

You running
From your

Brother
Chasing you

With a water
Gun—

Cool in the
Sun

The spray
Feels on

Your brown
Burning

Neck

Serenity Prayer with Complete Citations
After Julian Randall

Lord[1],
grant me the serenity[2] to accept the things
I cannot change[3], the courage to change
the things I can[4], and the wisdom
to know the difference[5]
Amen[6]

---

1   Name I'm taught to gift to any *higher power*. Prayer by way of substitution. I lord you—survival; future-girl; unopened bottle; rent check I don't vanish first into the gut & then the drain; light caught over the mist tongued horizon that looks, I imagine, like the inside of a wedding veil; pale glow the opposite of fluorescent; antonym of whitewashed concrete; antonym of perspex doors shuddered shut.

2   I never believed I would build from a room I was backed into. Court order that kept me breathing. I don't want to give them credit for this. As if the memory of that night hasn't also almost killed me.

3   The sentence. The angle of the collision. Eyes drifting shut behind the wheel. The number I called. The way the number changed the second time they breathalyzed me, when the first time I blew clean. How they rewrote the contents of my blood. How the booking officer refused me water for hours. How he stared. At my painted nails. At my painted lips. Mouthed *faggot* under his breath. How the shift ended & he logged his overtime.

4   I know that spite, too, can be a kind of god. I'm four years sober. Still learning not to panic when left alone in white rooms. I see a cop car a block away & my ears ring like a bronze AA token flipped through the air. I keep walking. Like doing this—while trans—couldn't get me questioned, cuffed, detained. Again.

5   Truth is, I don't know of any proper antonym for *jail*. Hence, my faith is an absence. My higher power—an unfilled mouth. A prayer is not what leaves my tongue, but that which I do not allow to enter me. Salvation is whatever word means I will not return there.

6   There is only one word that means the opposite of jail & it is *outside*. The first breath of open air. I walked out of a cell painted how I was told I should imagine heaven & every new place my feet touched was holy ground.

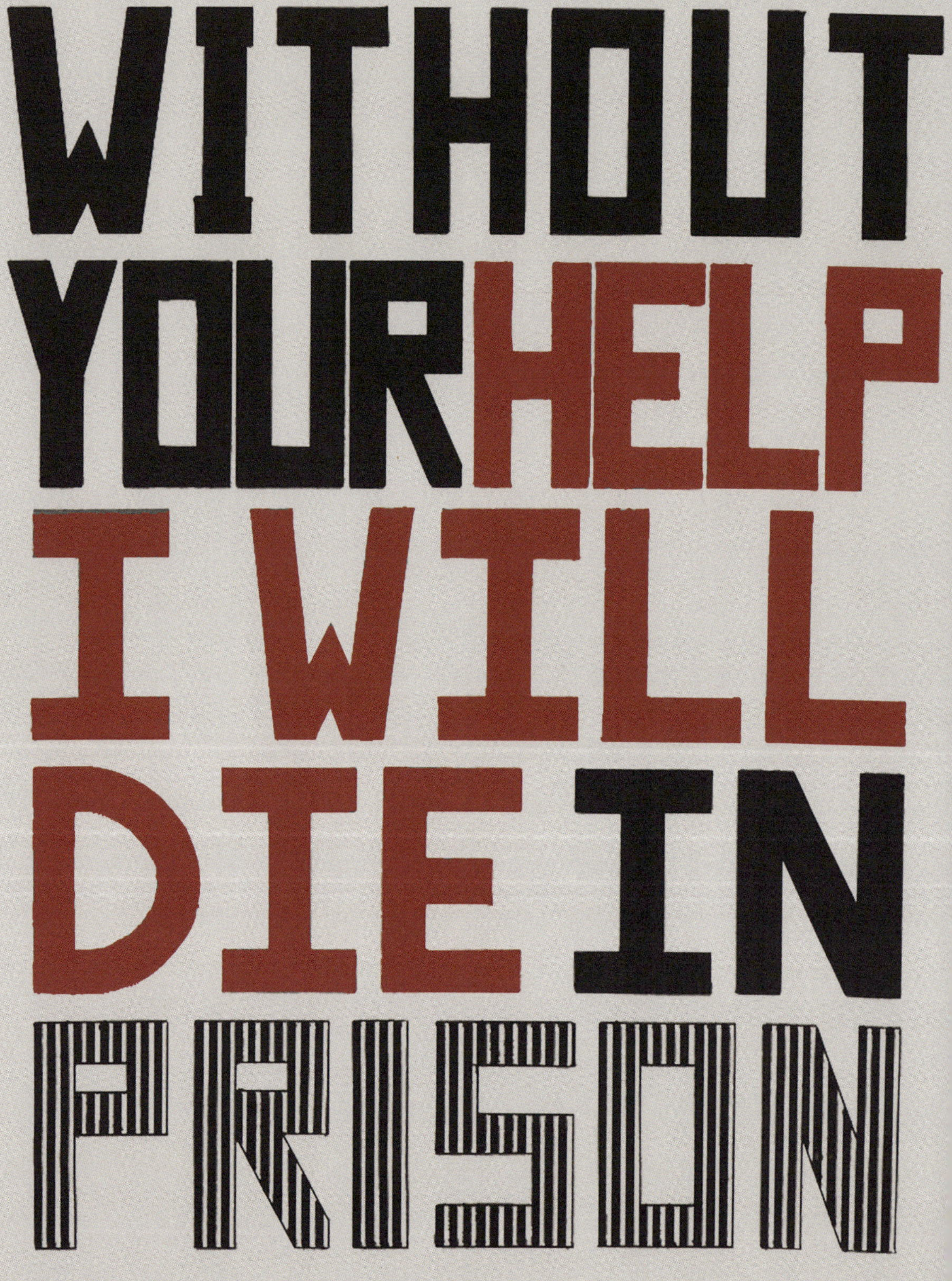

WITHOUT YOUR HELP I WILL DIE IN PRISON

WITHOUT YOUR HELP

WILL DIE IN PRISON

Alice Kim

"I FOLLOWED THE PHILOSOPHY OF HARRIET TUBMAN": AN INTERVIEW WITH RENALDO HUDSON

« Joseph Dole, *Without Your Help*, 2018 & *Without Your Help* _______, 2019

After 37 years behind bars, including 13 on death row, Renaldo Hudson came home when his life sentence was commuted to time served by Illinois Governor J.B. Pritzker. Renaldo's life took a dramatic turn while he was on death row, sentenced to die for taking another man's life during the course of an attempted robbery. Feeling both the weight of what he had done and his own humanity, Renaldo began a journey of atonement and personal transformation. He not only learned how to read, write and paint, he became a leader on the inside committed to building a more just and humane world.

I was an organizer with the Campaign to End the Death Penalty (CEDP) when I first met Renaldo in 1999 in the condemned unit visiting room at Pontiac Correctional Center, one of two prisons in Illinois where death row prisoners were caged. I remember being struck by Renaldo's candor and magnanimity. He refused to be defined by the worst act he had committed, and he refused to be silenced, openly admitting his guilt. At a time when politicians embraced and implemented a tough-on-crime agenda, and the media and even the anti-death penalty movement were almost exclusively focused on questions of innocence, Renaldo was a lone voice insisting that the "guilty" retained their humanity, rights, and were worthy of mercy.

In 2003, Renaldo's death sentence was commuted to life in prison without the possibility of parole (LWOP) by then Governor George Ryan who issued blanket commutations of 167 Illinois death sentences. A broad-based coalition had organized a yearlong campaign calling on the governor to commute all of the state's death sentences, and in a historic move, he responded to this demand. While many death penalty abolitionists celebrated this victory, Renaldo and his death row comrades understood that they had joined the ranks of "lifers" and now faced an in-house death sentence. Governor Ryan's justification of his decision to issue blanket commutations revealed this hard truth. "They will be confined in a cell that is 5 feet by 12 feet," he said.

"In summer months, the temperature gets as high as 100 degrees. It is a stark and dreary existence. Life without parole has even, at times, been described by prosecutors as a fate worse than death."[1]

With matter of fact foresight, prior to the governor's blanket commutations, Renaldo wrote to *The New Abolitionist*, the CEDP's national newsletter, in 2002, "Many understand that once they're off death row, they will fall into a bigger pool of hell within the prison system, where thousands of men and women are trying to find lawyers and support for their cases."[2] Although LWOP was deemed by some as a more humane alternative to capital punishment, increasingly advocates are insisting that death by incarceration is still cruel and unusual punishment and a clear violation of Article 5 of the Universal Declaration of Human Rights (UDHR).

In Illinois, of the more than 5,000 people serving life or de facto life sentences (50 or more years), 67 percent are Black, according to The Sentencing Project's 2017 report, "Still Life: America's Increasing Use of Life and Long-Term Sentences."[3] Illinois is also one of six states where all life sentences are imposed without the possibility of parole. Nationwide, more than 200,000 predominantly Black people are condemned to death by incarceration, effectively disappearing a section of the country's population into literal cages inside maximum-security prisons.

In my conversation with Renaldo, one week after he was released, he eloquently made the case that life sentences, like death sentences, are tantamount to legal lynching. In 1947, when W.E.B. Du Bois and the National Association for the Advancement of Colored People submitted their petition, "An Appeal to the World," to the newly established United Nations addressing the denial of human rights to Black Americans, they wrote: "People of the World, we American Negroes appeal to you; our treatment in America... is a basic problem of humanity; of democracy; of discrimination because of race and color... No nation is so great that the world can afford to let it continue to be deliberately unjust, cruel, and unfair toward its own citizens." Then, in 1951, the Civil Rights Congress filed the historic "We Charge Genocide" petition citing "killings by police, killings by incited gangs, killings at night by masked men, killings always on the basis of 'race,' killings by the Ku Klux Klan, that organization which is charted by several states as a semi-official arm of government and even granted the tax exemptions of a benevolent society." The petition explicitly names "the thousands of Negroes who over the years have been beaten to death on chain gangs and in the backrooms of sheriff's offices, in the cells of county jails, in precinct police stations and on city streets, who have been framed and murdered by sham legal forms and by a legal bureaucracy." Now, in 2020, we can add life sentences to the egregious list of human rights violations.

In this interview, Renaldo shares what his first days of freedom looked like, how he survived both a death sentence and life without the possibility of parole, and the inhumanity of death by incarceration.

—

Alice Kim: *Welcome home. It's amazing that you're out now, here with us, that you're home after 37 long years. What has this first week out been like for you, what has been surprising to you?*

Renaldo Hudson: Oh man, everything. Well, the most obvious thing that everyone's been teasing me about is the phone, like the amount of information. I've been talking to the phone and even the computer now, right? I'll give you a perfect example. It's the funniest thing to me. The other day, I said, "Google, call my mama" and Google said to me, "Who is your mama?" And that's something that was so cool. I just tried it, you know, and it didn't work, but it was just funny to me.

The other thing is, I went downtown to the lakefront, and so I'm walking on the lakefront and I'm really close to the water, and I can hear the water hitting close. And it sounded to me like freedom. It brought me to tears. To be perfectly honest with you, I watered up because I realized in that moment, how free I really was.

I get that. And I wonder, what do you want the world to know about your journey from death row to life in prison without the possibility of parole, to now being out and finally gaining your freedom? Darby Tillis used to say, "I was released from death row, but I am not free of death row because it will always be with me." Do you feel similarly?

I will not echo that sentiment because I do not think death row will always be with me. I am not my sentence. Being here right now is a testament to that fact—that I was sentenced to die, but that was not my destiny. I refuse to be defined by that. I want the world to know that there's life in me, that there's love in me, that I want to share for the rest of my life what a person that's determined to be better looks like. You know, I want to tell my story in a way that does not glamorize the process.

A lot of people will look at the crime that I committed, and those are the cracks that make me imperfect. You may see my cracks, but they're just an indicator of my trauma, which leaves me open for change.

I want the world to know that I'm so much better than the bad decision that I made over 37 years ago, and I'm remorseful for it. I'm sorry that I wasn't a better human being. Today I'm sober. Today, I've taken ownership of all that, not just parts, you know? And I think people need to know that there's so many more Renaldos locked in prison who will not get a chance to say I'm sorry because the adversarial system that we're in does not reward confession. I remember how many people said, "Renaldo, you is so stupid, stop confessing. They'll never let you out." And so many people wrote me off, right? But I've always believed that there has to be a voice for those of us that are actually guilty. And people have to know that there are people that are willing to attempt to make atonement and use their platform to say, "Hey, listen, you can heal from this, you can be better than that one incident or however many it was, and you can own it." I don't minimize it. I always tell people, "Listen, Mr. Folke Peterson deserved so much better than what my life brought into his life."

At the same time, the mitigating versus the aggravating have to be laid out. Every day people talk about profiling without going into people's history. Like what went wrong with Renaldo Hudson? I'm simply saying to people, "Yes, you can talk about the crime," like when the article came out in the *Tribune* ["From death row to model inmate, Renaldo Hudson set free after 37 years. 'I was preparing to die. I wasn't preparing for this moment'"] the other day, and I went on Facebook and some people were talking really, really crazy [saying], "He's a monster, and he committed a horrible crime." And I said to myself, you're absolutely correct that I committed a horrible crime. But I'm not a monster. I'm a human being that made a really bad decision, you know? I'm looking to be a part of a society of broken people. Maybe I'm the only one broken, but I'm willing to confess mine. Everything about Renaldo Hudson is public, so how are you going to shame me about how much of a monster you think I am when my story has already been told for years? And so I'm really wanting to use whatever platform I have to say to people that we've left a lot of good people in prison, male and female. I want to be a part of helping to bring some of those people back out here, so that the testimony is not limited and cut off at the Renaldo Hudson story.

Absolutely. I want to get into the question of life without the possibility of parole as a human rights violation because it's not always seen as one. Let's go back to Governor Ryan's historic commutations. It was a heated topic on death row and on the outside, and I recall all the conversations we had while we were engaged in the battle for commutations. And ultimately, it was a bittersweet victory. That's how we described it. Execution by the state was now off the table for those whose sentences were commuted, but people were now facing life without the possibility of parole, which we called an in-house death sentence. Can you talk about what it meant to be facing LWOP?

I am so glad you brought this subject up because it's really one of my pet peeves. The scripture teaches me as a theologian, hope deferred makes the heart sick. And to tell someone, you never have a day of hope, are you serious? Like you're gonna send me off to the penitentiary and say don't ever hope of having hope because we've taken that from you. You're not going to kill me, you're going to wait for me to die. I still have a death sentence, but we're gonna do you the courtesy of just waiting and let you suffer."

No one should be placed in a state of mind in which they have no hope. To put anyone in a position of not having hope is a human rights violation. You're telling me there's nothing redeemable about me. That I don't matter. The inhumanity of having a life sentence is that you don't belong to yourself. You're telling me that the only way my family will have possession of me again is through me dying. But I was never rocked to sleep. I'm like, "Man, you got to keep fighting, because they will wait for you to die, and they'll have the audacity to call your people and say, 'You can have the body now.'" That's torture.

The inhumanity of having a life sentence is that you don't even belong to yourself. You belong to [corrections]. How could that not be a human rights violation? Because that's equal to slavery. You're telling me I can never have independence again for the rest of my life. That sounds a whole lot like slavery to me. But other than that, you're gonna make me work for slave wages. Right? That's if you let me work, because I have this natural life sentence. Right, because a natural life sentence also says to you that you don't get privileges, like even getting some type of education. Perfect example, when Governor Ryan commuted my sentence to life without parole, I went to Stateville. I did not have a GED. I immediately saw the school line and I was like, "Hey, what's this?" So I sent a request slip in and they said to me, "Oh, you have too much time but we'll put you on the list. But you need to understand that every time someone comes to the prison with a lesser sentence, you'll go to the bottom of the list again."

And so when you talk about the human rights violation of having natural life, it comes in so many dimensions. When an officer comes to my cell, and I have a life sentence, they are immediately placed in a hostile state because they say you can't trust me because, "Hey, you have life without parole. I heard about you. You're never going home." Now imagine trying to have a conversation with someone and trying to have a decent day and they're saying, "Oh, yeah, that's one of them lifers. He's never going home, I'll retire before he leaves."

If you're going to address the issue of the death penalty and capital punishment, then natural life without parole has to be included because it's just an extension. Instead of them saying, "This is the day you're going to be executed," they're saying, "We're satisfied with the day that you die," right?

I watched every execution that occurred on death row from Charlie Walker, who was the first execution since the death penalty was reinstated, to the last execution of a guy by the name of Andrew Kokoraleis. Every execution, I turned my television off, I turned my radio off, and I said, "Lord have mercy." They tried to appease us—it was the weirdest thing in the world. They brought us special meals during every execution. Like, "Okay, could you give me some extra cookies and an extra piece of chicken, and you think I'm going to forget you just took a guy out and executed him," you know?

Listen, Alice, when they sentenced me to life without parole, I'll be honest with you, I was personally heartbroken that there was no one standing and saying, "Hey, this is an injustice." Everyone was celebrating the release of the few people that got released, and God bless them, I've never been envious of anyone else's release; I celebrated it. But my heart was breaking because I knew that there was a different fight that was occurring.

You're so right, Renaldo. I mean, it was at once this completely historic thing that happened and then at the same time, it was heartbreaking. I remember talking to people [on death row] immediately after that happened, and these were not happy conversations because now there was this sense of doom because people now had life sentences. The bitter irony was that you had a lawyer assigned to you when you were on death row, you had your own cell, and you had an abolitionist movement standing up for you. I remember how fearful folks were of being lost in this sea of mass incarceration.

I'll give you a quick example of one of the things I know you remember. When

Governor Ryan commuted us, the attorney general of the State of Illinois attempted to send me back to death row.

I remember.

I was at Stateville because they moved us to population. News reporters were waiting to see what would happen. And so they set up an interview when they expected the decision to come down, and they had all these questions about what if they send you back to death row. What are you going to do? What are you thinking? How are your feelings? But here's the thing that goes to your question about natural life without the possibility of parole: the moment they discovered that my life sentence would be sustained, they no longer wanted to have a conversation. It was really, really something that stuck with me. I'm like, "Man, so you're telling me you wanted to talk to me when you thought I was completely condemned, but throw him on an island and just wait for him to die, and that's okay?" That wasn't even news. Think about that. Having life without the possibility of parole [was] not even newsworthy. So even if you just look back at that little moment, how could I ever expect someone to want to hear my story when people don't even deem it worthy of a conversation. There are not any news reporters knocking the doors down saying, "Listen, we have X amount of people with actual legal death dates sitting in penitentiaries." I want to be a part of the platform that begins to awaken people to this horror.

[After Gov Ryan's commutations] there was a tremendous amount of desperation, there was a tremendous amount of distress. Like, what are we going to do now? Who's going to take on our plight now? I had to face the possibility that I would never, ever, ever walk out of prison. Hopeless people do crazy things, and I want to be a part of people having hope, you know? Life without parole doesn't leave hope. You make people time bombs.

Right. So let's talk about Article 5 of the UDHR, which directly pertains to incarceration. Article 5 asserts that no one shall be subjected to torture or to cruel, inhumane, or degrading treatment or punishment. How do you define cruel, inhumane, or degrading punishment?

Here's what I've learned, that cruel and unusual punishment could be for one person way to the left of the spectrum and to others way to the right. I met a guy that had a year and a day as his sentence. He did a year in the county jail, so he had to go to prison for one day. He went to his cell and hung himself. But before he hung himself, he said, "I can't take it. It's too much." The pressure of one day in prison was too much for him. He was so tortured by his fear of prison.

Prison produces psychological torture. And we now know psychological torture is just as harmful as physical torture. Will I ever see my mother? Will I ever see my daughter? Will I ever breathe a different kind of air? I'm noticing how much fresher the air is on this side. I'm serious. Everything is brighter, the colors.

Every day of my incarceration was torturous. Every day of my incarceration was painful. I may not act like it was. That's because I'm strong. You know, I was made to fight. I wasn't made to wither away, but every day, every second of incarceration is torturous. If you don't let a person see an end to it, people will lose their mind thinking about it.

People need to know the real story and how ugly it really is to be put into a penitentiary and told you will never walk outta here. You know? I said to my lawyer, Jennifer Soble, I used to say to her, "Man, please don't let me die in prison." And she said, "I'm not gonna let you die in prison. We're going to get you out." I heard the hurt in her voice that I had to make that plea, but I wanted her to understand what I was feeling. Does that make sense?

It makes a lot of sense. Joseph Dole, who's incarcerated at Stateville, is a co-founder of Parole Illinois. He made this graphic that says, "Without your help—blank space—will die in prison." The blank space is so that you can write in the name of your loved one who's serving a life or virtual life sentence. I had just printed out copies of the graphic one day, and Ronnie Kitchen [who was on death row with Renaldo] came by my office right around that time. We wrote your name in and we took this photo. With these graphics, we're trying to make the same point to the media, to legislators, to the public: don't let our loved ones die in prison. It's not okay to lock people up and throw away the key.

Exactly. Until people begin to realize that we need help, like don't just condemn people and throw them in a hole. We've been friends for years, right? Real talk. Did you think I would ever walk out of prison?

You know, I honestly didn't know. I thought it took a lot of courage for you to openly admit guilt, drop your legal appeals, and go for clemency instead.

I have always wanted to ask you about that, because if you want to be true to yourself and live your truth—like you did—you have to make a decision that might hurt your chances of getting out. Our legal system is so unforgiving and adversarial. But I always felt that because you're the one who has to walk in those shoes, you're the only one who has the authority to make those kinds of decisions—and it's not for any of us to judge. Can you talk about how you came to choose this strategy for freedom?

When I made the decision, it was like this decision versus the world. And I was like, "Man, no one's seeing what I see." You know, there's a lot of things that had to come together. I received a lot of no's. I seen people just move on and say, "You know what, Renaldo is done for." And so I'm humbled that people chose to stay, and I love the way you put it, like, hey, you have to make a decision that you think you can live with. And I knew I could live with it. And then the other side of it, there are so many people who feel like we never own our stuff. And I'm like, I'm all in. I was the most guilty person that you could meet the day I was arrested, and the first thing my lawyer said to me was, "Shhh," or the police, "You have the right to remain silent, anything you say can and will be used against you in a court of law." I think about how crazy our system is. The very thing that they're trained to do, they're trained to undo in the same breath. If that's not the craziest thing in the world. You tell me I have a Miranda right, but then you train people on how to maneuver around the right to be silent. And then we see it every day in the police stations. "Hey, send Billy in there. He's the best at getting them to confess." Our system is so broken when people get a chance to actually see it for what it really is.

Another way of thinking about the system is that it's not actually broken, it's doing exactly what it was designed to do. We used to say the death penalty system was broken, but then we had to say, wait a minute, it's actually doing what it's supposed to do. And same with the criminal punishment system. And so that's what we need to expose and insist that we don't need to live in this way. We don't need to have a world where we have prisons. Everything that you've been talking about, your life and the decisions that you made after your conviction, shows that we can't be defined by the worst thing that we've ever done. People do have the capacity to change and to live completely different lives. And you know, the world is a better place with you in it, with you being out here with us. Isn't that the world that we want?

I knew that if I planted those seeds, at some point they would produce a harvest, you know? And that's what people don't understand. Like everything has to manifest of itself. I just believe that. And life has proven it to me. Going back to what you asked me, I believed it was the best decision. I now know that it was the right decision for me. It just took more time, a lot of time.

How did you maintain and sustain all those years?

I sustained on multiple levels. On a personal level, I knew that I had to protect my heart, and when I say my heart, I'm talking about my mind. I began to feed myself, like I read a lot of books, a lot of revolutionary books. People don't know, they saw my smile but they didn't know that I was in war mode. I was reading war generals. I read great leaders. Abraham Lincoln, Roosevelt, Lyndon B. Johnson, modern day leaders. I read about the anatomy of governments. I was reading about the structure of government and what a good government should look like. And those books showed me that my government that I was subject to was corrupt and it was eroding away before our very eyes because it was saying to its citizens, "We will condemn you."

I'm a man of faith, I pray to my God, but I don't beat people up with my faith, but it works for me. So I started to pray. I started to meditate. They just made you mad, they just did this to you, came to your cell, and just stripped all your stuff out and molested it. "OK, do not respond to them." It took a lot of restraint. I was a grown man and I was watching an academy of cadets, fresh out of high school, and all of a sudden, you're coming to tell me to shut up, inmate. You're nothing. So I had to say, you know what, I have a tough mind, but a soft heart. And so I worked on being tough. You're not going to hurt my feelings. Because I don't love the system. A lot of my peers, began to value themselves based upon their positions in the prison system. And I never allowed myself to do that—even though I worked [in the prison]. I always maintained a mental distance to where I could say I'm going to keep my integrity.

I followed the philosophy of Harriet Tubman even before I got out of prison. I was like, "I'm going to get out and I'm going to bring some people out with me."

I was training. I was studying. I was reading. I read so many books on leadership, so many books on getting from here to there. And I'll be really, really honest, I stopped blaming other people for my state. My brother shot me at 15 and my other brother killed my twin, and, man, my life is so miserable, and I don't know my dad and my father died and my mother died and my granddaddy died. You can begin to just dig your own grave.

Prisons are like graveyards where dreams die, spirits die. I knew I wouldn't die in prison and it's because I developed my brain. Education is crucially important in the fight to survive and to maintain your humanity. Because they are connected. Education and humanity are connected. Human rights violations start by them allowing people to be illiterate in prison.

It's a human right to be educated. That was the main thing about slavery: don't teach them how to read because reading frees you. Once the light comes on, it's hard to hide.

Yes, education needs to be understood as a human right. Article 3 of the UDHR also says, "Everyone has the right to life, liberty, and security of person." What does that mean for someone who's incarcerated? How does it speak to you as someone who spent nearly 40 years incarcerated?

I think the hardest thing to do is showing that even when a person is guilty, you don't lose your humanity because you're guilty. This speaks to me because society has to be reminded that you have to be better than the broken person that is standing in front of you. You can't act like the broken person and say this is justice. Even the guilty still have their humanity. And there's a duty that you still have even to the guilty.

Can you say more about our duty to the guilty?

Look at my life story as an example. What made me take the position that I take and talk about the guilty is because I never lost my humanity. I made a bad decision. And society somehow tried to make me think that my humanity left me with a crime. That was a crime that I'm responsible for, but that's a moment in my life. That is not my life. I'm responsible for it. I paid a price for it. I think it was excessive. At the age of 19, I had the mental capacity of a 13-year-old. Anyone that looked at that case and really looked at me saw this was a very disturbed teenager that made a horrible, horrible decision. Now that being said, it was a shame that people that knew better understood that that was a crazy, impulsive bad decision. Instead of them saying, "Now, let's see if we can kind of find out what went wrong," they took the route of "how can we show this person to be so monstrous we can justify eliminating their life, taking their life from them?" And it's a sport—it wasn't justice when

I was sentenced. It was a part of a sport of judges and state's attorneys.

I was such a non-person to them. I didn't have a family that would be in their faces. I didn't have the support other than the public defender's office. You know when I went to trial, my lawyers bought the clothes that I sat in front of the jury in. So I didn't have no one to actually fight for me. That's why I knew that I had to learn how to fight for myself. And in fighting for myself, my humanity was awakened because it was never taken from me. It just went dormant. But it was awakened. I'm like, "Wait a minute. How many more Renaldo's are there that are guilty but our stories are not being told?" Our stories have to be told. What went wrong with this kid? If you look at every guilty person, somewhere there's a misfire, something not triggering right, and people don't want to investigate that. That's why I think it's important that the guilty start talking, even though we're trained not to.

The legal system does not actually value truth, right?

Yes. Exactly, and that's what makes my story so strong, because the legal system fought so hard against me trying to be truthful. They wanted to turn me into a liar, and then uncover the lie.

Alright, let's turn to Charles McLaurin's prints featured in this book. He was on death row with you and, like you, his sentence was also commuted to LWOP. He made prints based on the following articles from the UDHR.
- *Everyone has the right to freedom of thought, conscience, and religion.*
- *Everyone has the right to freedom of peaceful assembly and association. No one may be compelled to belong to an association.*
- *Everyone has the right to freely participate in the cultural life of the community, to enjoy the arts, and to share in scientific advancement and its benefits.*
What do they say to you?

Well, all of them kind of speak to me in a personal way because I love art. Art helps to free people even while incarcerated. There's a tremendous amount of freedom when you can say what you want to say with your art, do what you want to do with it. Prison may restrict the tools you use to express yourself, but it can't restrict your expression. And one of the things that I say about Charles McLaurin is he's showing in his heart his willingness to fight against feeling imprisoned. I love that in every one of his pieces. You can walk through his art and say, "Ah, I get it," you know, from education to community service. What I see is the pain of his struggle to be heard in the midst of so much noise. That's probably the painful part of art is when you see restrained art as an expression from an artist.

What do you mean by restrained art?

His art is expressing a clear thought but I can see how restrained it is coming out of a prison setting. It's clear to me he wanted to say more to the subject because I've been in his position. So he had to speak in an abstract or non-direct way. If given the chance to be in a free place, this expression would change completely. You can interpret it any way you want to.

Look at this picture here [indicates McLaurin's print *Article 27* on pp. 116-117]. You see him holding this book up, but who holds a book like this? Hands up. I'm like, "Don't shoot." Then when you see the stripes, some people would say, "I see the sun," right? I see bars, like I see the restraints of prison holding the group of people in restraints.

I love what you're sharing about what you see in the work and the art itself. As we bring this to a close, any last words?

When you sit in a prison cell with life without parole, you're made to believe that you're worthless. I'll be honest with you, knowing that they were attempting to strip all my humanity from me, it made me want to fight. It made me say, "You know what? No, you're not going to win this fight." It's just remembering and understanding how much, how much it costs. It costs to be an activist. It costs to be a voice for people. And my tears is not because I'm sad, it's because I'm happy. I'm happy that I know that I have a life and that my life is worth something.

---

1   Robert E. Pierre and Kari Lydersen, "Illinois Death Row Emptied," *The Washington Post*, January 12, 2003, https://www.washingtonpost.com/archive/politics/2003/01/12/illinois-death-row-emptied/4b875452-2b99-4616-8394-6fc7e9798408/.

2   Chicago Torture Victims, *Tortured by Blue* (Bloomington, IN: Balboa Press, 2019).

3   Ashley Nellis, *Still Life: America's Increasing Use of Life and Long-Term Sentences* (Washington DC: The Sentencing Project, 2017), 14, https://www.sentencingproject.org/publications/still-life-americas-increasing-use-life-long-term-sentences/.

Photo by Alice Kim, 2020 [Ronnie Kitchen holding a *Without Your Help* sign by Joseph Dole for Renaldo Hudson.] »

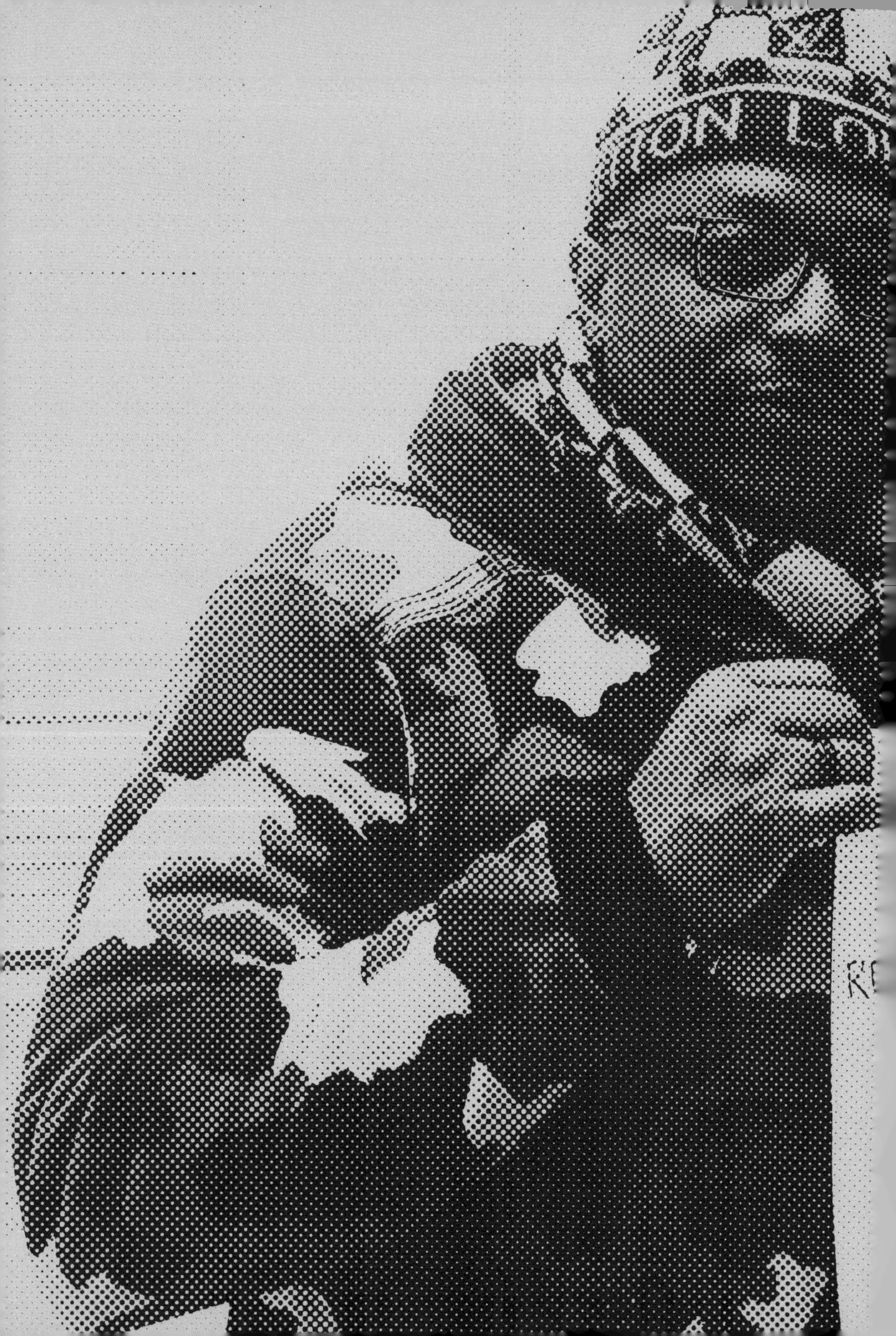

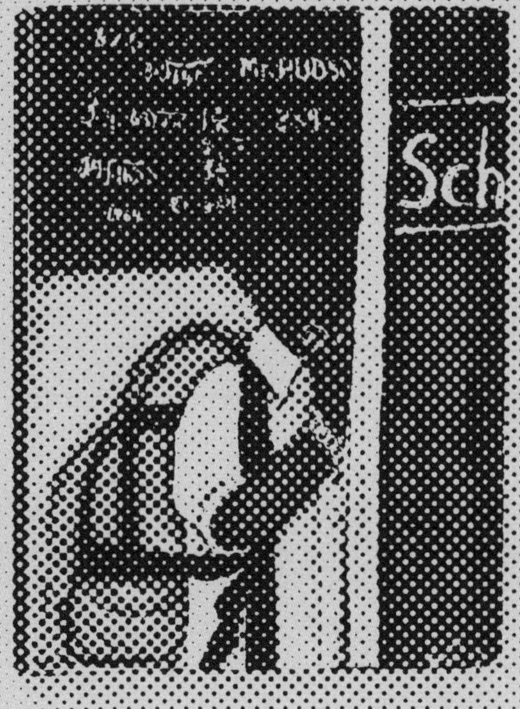

THOUT
RHELP

HUDSON

LL
IN

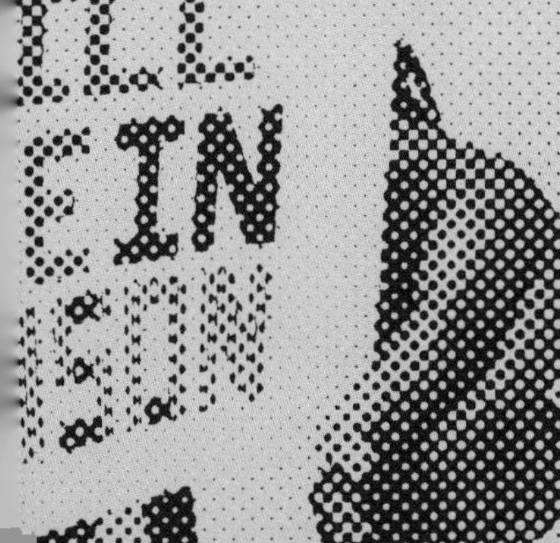

Poem for July 4, 1994
For President Václav Havel

1.

It is essential that Summer be grafted to
bones marrow earth clouds blood the
eyes of our ancestors.
It is essential to smell the beginning
words where Washington, Madison, Hamilton,
Adams, Jefferson assembled amid cries of:

"The people lack of information"
"We grow more and more skeptical"
"This Constitution is a triple-headed monster"
"Blacks are property"

It is essential to remember how cold the sun
how warm the snow snapping
around the ragged feet of soldiers and slaves.
It is essential to string the sky
with the saliva of Slavs and
Germans and Anglos and French
and Italians and Scandinavians,
and Spaniards and Mexicans and Poles
and Africans and Native Americans.
It is essential that we always repeat:
we the people,
we the people,
we the people.

"Let us go into the fields" one
brother told the other brother. And
the sound of exact death
raising tombs across the centuries.
Across the oceans. Across the land.

It is essential that we finally understand:
this is the time for the creative
human being
the human being who decides
to walk upright in a human
fashion in order to save this
earth from extinction.

This is the time for the creative
Man. Woman. Who must decide
that She. He. Can live in peace.
Racial and sexual justice on
this earth.

This is the time for you and me.
African American. Whites. Latinos.
Gays. Asians. Jews. Native
Americans. Lesbians. Muslims.
All of us must finally bury
the elitism of race superiority
the elitism of sexual superiority

the elitism of economic superiority
the elitism of religious superiority.

So we welcome you on the celebration
of 218 years Philadelphia. America.

So we salute you and say:
Come, come, come, move out into this world
nourish your lives with a
spirituality that allows us to respect
each other's birth.
come, come, come, nourish the world where
every 3 days 120,000 children die
of starvation or the effects of starvation;
come, come, come, nourish the world
where we will no longer hear the
screams and cries of women, girls,
and children in Bosnia, El Salvador,
Rwanda ... AhAhAhAh AHAHAHHHHH

      Ma-ma. Dada. Mamacita. Baba.
      Mama. Papa. Momma. Poppi.
      The soldiers are marching in the streets
      near the hospital but the nurses say
      we are safe and the soldiers are
      laughing marching firing calling
      out to us i don't want to die i
      am only 9 yrs old, i am only 10 yrs old
      i am only 11 yrs old and i cannot
      get out of the bed because they have cut
      off one of my legs and i hear the soldiers
      coming toward our rooms and i hear
      the screams and the children are
      running out of the room and i can't get out
      of the bed i don't want to die Don't
      let me die Rwanda. America. United
      Nations. Don't let me die ....

Sonia Sanchez

And if we nourish ourselves, our communities
our countries and say

        no more hiroshima
        no more auschwitz
        no more wounded knee
        no more middle passage
        no more slavery
        no more Bosnia
        no more Rwanda

No more intoxicating ideas of
racial superiority
as we walk toward abundance
we will never forget

        the earth
        the sea
        the children
        the people

For *we the people* will always be arriving
a ceremony of thunder
waking up the earth
opening our eyes to human
monuments.
    And it'll get better
    it'll get better
if *we the people* work, organize, resist,
come together for peace, racial, social
and sexual justice
    it'll get better
    it'll get better.

Ode to the Soccer Ball Sailing Over a Barbed Wire Fence

> *Tornillo... has become the symbol of what may be the largest U.S. mass*
> *detention of children not charged with crimes since the World War II*
> *internment of Japanese-Americans.*
>
> —Robert Moore, *Texas Monthly*

Praise *Tornillo*: word for screw in Spanish, word for *jailer* in English,
word for three thousand adolescent migrants incarcerated in camp.

Praise the three thousand soccer balls gift-wrapped at Christmas,
as if raindrops in the desert inflated and bounced through the door.

Praise the soccer games rotating with a whistle every twenty minutes
so three thousand adolescent migrants could take turns kicking a ball.

Praise the boys and girls who walked a thousand miles, blood caked
in their toes, yelling in Spanish and a dozen Mayan tongues on the field.

Praise the first teenager, brain ablaze like chili pepper Christmas lights,
to kick a soccer ball high over the chain link and barbed wire fence.

Praise the first teenager to scrawl a name and number on the face
of the ball, then boot it all the way to the dirt road on the other side.

Praise the smirk of teenagers at the jailers scooping up fugitive
soccer balls, jabbering about the ingratitude of teenagers at Christmas.

Praise the soccer ball sailing over the barbed wire fence, white
and black like the moon, yellow like the sun, blue like the world.

Praise the soccer ball flying to the moon, flying to the sun, flying to other
worlds, flying to Antigua Guatemala, where Starbucks buys coffee beans.

Praise the soccer ball bounding off the lawn at the White House,
thudding off the president's head as he waves to absolutely no one.

Praise the piñata of the president's head, jellybeans pouring from his ears,
enough to feed three thousand adolescents incarcerated at Tornillo.

Praise *Tornillo*: word in Spanish for adolescent migrant internment camp,
abandoned by jailers in the desert, liberated by a blizzard of soccer balls.

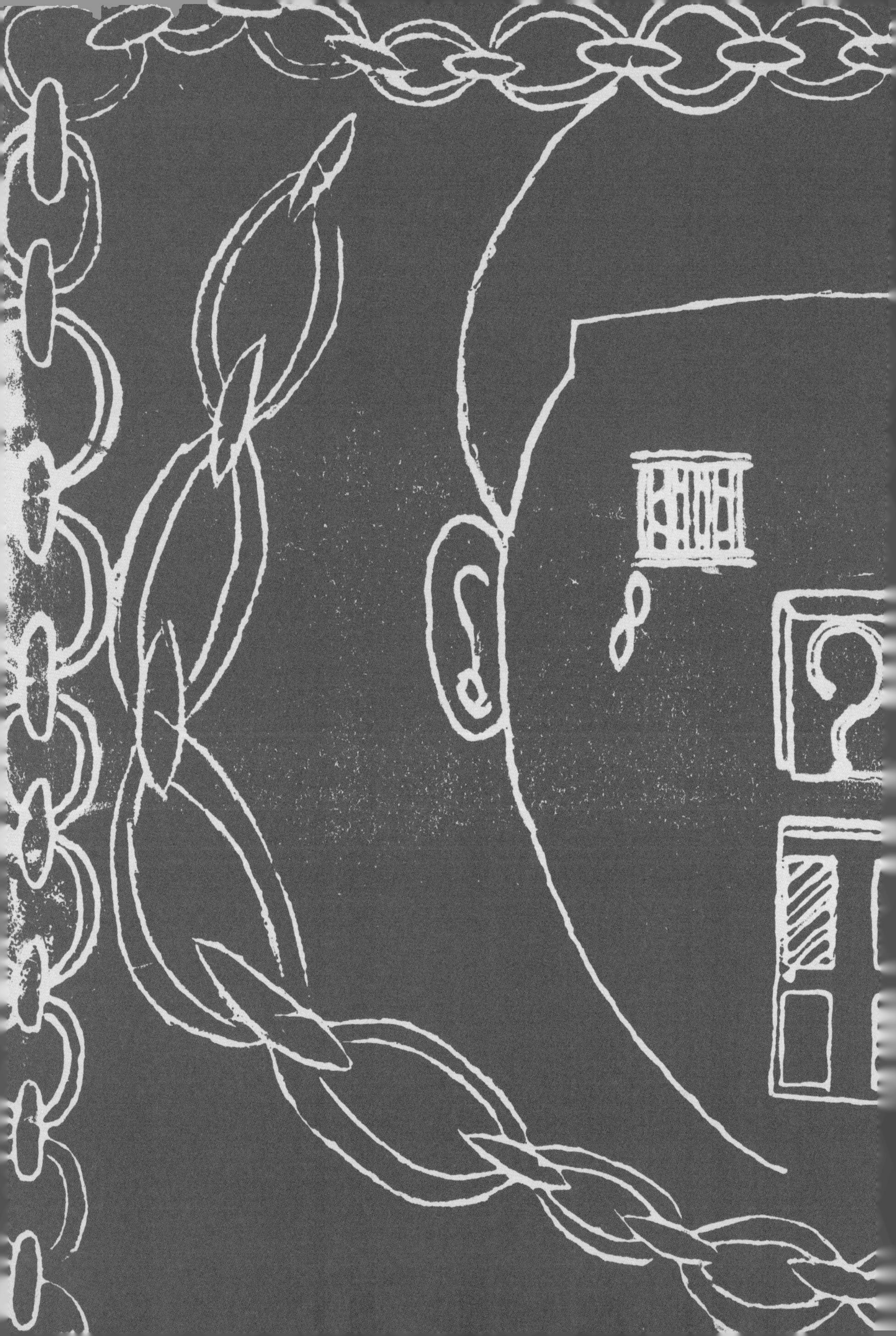

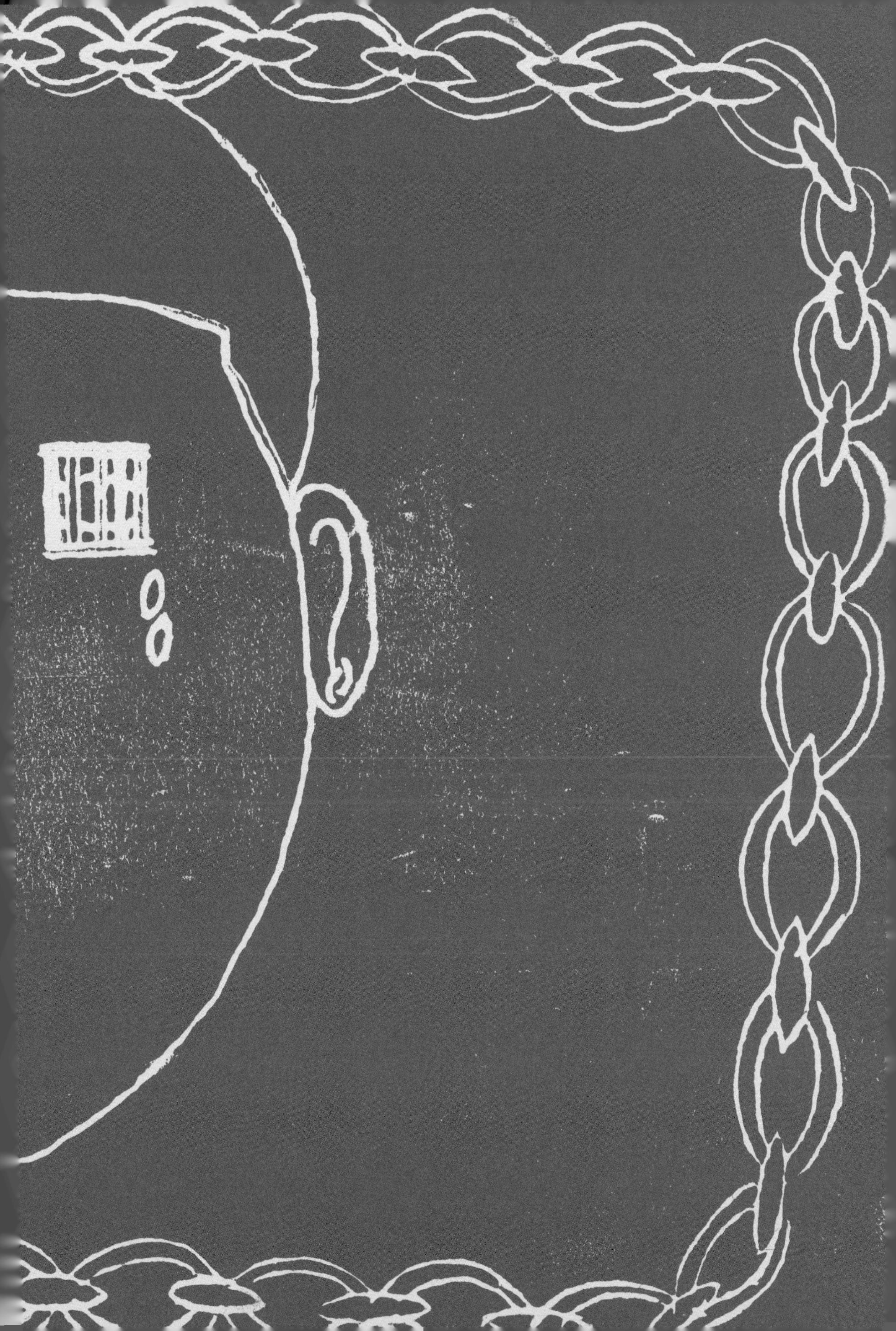

Benny Rios Donjuan

ARE RIGHTS TRULY SELF-EVIDENT?

« Robert Boyd, *Face*, 2016

*Somewhere we must come to see that human progress never rolls
in on the wheels of inevitability. It comes through the tireless efforts
and the persistent work of dedicated individuals who are willing
to be co-workers with God. And without this hard work, time itself
becomes an ally of the primitive forces of social stagnation. So
we must help time and realize that the time is always ripe to do
right.*[1]

— Dr. Martin Luther King Jr.
"Remaining Awake Through the Great Revolution"

Three historical documents claim that the rights of people are self-evident:
the American Declaration of Independence, the French Declaration of the
Rights of Man and Citizen, and the United Nations Universal Declaration
of Human Rights. They all have almost the same things in common: that
all people are created equal and that we have rights to life, liberty, and the
pursuit of happiness. In *Inventing Human Rights: A History*, historian
Lynn Hunt writes,

> *Despite their differences in language the two 18th-century decla-
> rations both rested on a claim of self-evidence. Jefferson made this
> explicit when he wrote, 'We hold these truths to be self-evident.'
> The French declaration stated categorically, 'ignorance, neglect,
> or contempt of the rights of man are the sole cause of public mis-
> fortunes and governmental corruption.' Not much had changed in
> this regard by 1948.*[2]

Here, Hunt ties in all three historical documents and refers to the United
Nations Universal Declaration of Human Rights, signed in 1948.

What does it mean for something to be self-evident? According to the American Heritage Dictionary "self-evident" means "Requiring no proof or explanation." When these declarations were written I suppose that the definition pretty much held the same meaning. However, I have to ask the question... are rights truly self-evident? To answer that question, we don't have to search very far because throughout history, our rights—that are supposed to be self-evident—have been challenged and redefined over and over again. If the rights of all human beings are self-evident, why are there so many paradoxes, contradictions, different interpretations, and experiences of our so-called rights?

"All men are created equal." There really doesn't seem to be a need for interpretation of that statement but, unfortunately, that is far from true. Our founding fathers believed in that statement, yet they were slave owners and didn't consider enslaved Black people as fully human. "All men are created equal" didn't apply to Blacks and Native Americans in the United States when the Declaration of Independence was written; in fact, it only applied to white men who owned property. Even white women, who might have benefited from other privileges, were deprived of their rights. It took people like Frederick Douglass, a former enslaved person who became a social reformer, abolitionist, and orator, to bring light to the fact that, yes, indeed, Black people were created equal in the eyes of God. Women like Elizabeth Cady Stanton, an early activist for women's rights, worked closely with Lucretia Motts, a well-known abolitionist. Both women suffered oppression from white men that deprived them of their rights. These leaders worked together in the mid- to late- 1800s to fight for their rights as human beings so that they could have the same equal opportunities as white men. They spoke against the atrocities of slavery, the oppression of Black people, and exposed the ways white women were also denied rights as human beings. These leaders helped redefine the meaning of rights and who they applied to. Their victories were great, but they only scratched the surface for the battles yet to come.

In Frederick Douglass' speech, "What to the Slave is the Fourth of July?," one line stood out to me: "America is false to the past, false to the present, and solemnly binds herself to be false to the future."[3] This statement referred to leaders who had trampled on the Constitution and the Bible in order to promote evil and perpetuate slavery. Douglass was able to see far into the future to know that America would always be false to herself and that true freedom, fairness, and equal rights for everyone would be an ongoing battle.

Since that time, many more activists have risen to challenge white supremacy and racial injustices and to fight for both economic and human rights. Leaders such as Martin Luther King Jr., with the non-violent movement for civil rights; Cesar Chavez and the United Farm Workers movement; and 21st century activists with Occupy Wall Street and Black Lives Matter achieved victories, yet policies rooted in anti-Black racism, vicious laws against immigrants, and violence against poor, differently abled, or trans and queer people continue in full force today. What's more is that when victories are won, the state claims success, creating an illusion that the work is done. This is why full rights for everyone are not self-evident, rather what is, is the on-going struggle for them.

In 1988 the law scholar Kimberlé Crenshaw wrote an important article that looked at the limits of anti-discrimination law and civil rights for Black people in America. Crenshaw says,

> *Black people have been created as a subordinated 'other,' and formal reform has merely repackaged racism ... laws have largely succeeded in eliminating the symbolic manifestation of racial oppression, but have allowed the perpetuation of material subordination of Blacks.*[4]

In the criminal legal system, we are often led to believe that there is no racism or inequality in the legislative process and that laws are passed in the name of fairness. However, many times throughout history what was created was a legalized way to continue economic inequality and racial injustice.

From the era of Frederick Douglass up to today, one of the ways to challenge the institution of white supremacy internally has been by using its own logic against it. As Crenshaw says,

> *Such a crisis occurs when powerless people force open and politicize a contradiction between the dominant ideology and their reality ... the race neutrality of the legal system creates the illusion that racism is no longer the primary factor responsible for the condition of the Black underclass; instead, as we have seen, class disparities appear to be the consequence of individual and group merit within a supposed system of opportunity.*[5]

I believe this applies not only to Black people but to all people of color. When it comes down to it, people of color will have to depend on the rhetoric of rights in order to challenge the institution of white supremacy and protect our interests. We face an ongoing battle for our human rights.

There's no doubt that our rights are limited, making their self-evidence, once again, questionable. Our rights are trampled on, restricted, and regulated, just as politicians insist that we have equal rights. Nonetheless, we have come a very long way in fighting for what is right and for human rights. As we continue this struggle, we must renew and refresh the ways in which we work together and fight for human rights for all.

1   Martin Luther King, Jr., *A Knock At Midnight: Inspiration from the Great Sermons of Reverend Martin Luther King, Jr.* (New York: Warner Books, 1998), 201-225.
2   Lynn Hunt, *Inventing Human Rights: A History* (New York: W.W. Norton and Company, 2007), 19.
3   Frederick Douglass, "What to the Slave Is the Fourth of July?" in *Frederick Douglass: Selected Speeches and Writings*, ed. Philip S. Foner (Chicago: Lawrence Hill, 1999), 188-206.
4   Kimberlé Crenshaw, "Race, Reform, and Retrenchment: Transformation and Legitimation in Antidiscrimination Law," *Harvard Law Review*, Vol. 101 Number 7 (1988), 1331.
5   Crenshaw, "Race," 1383.

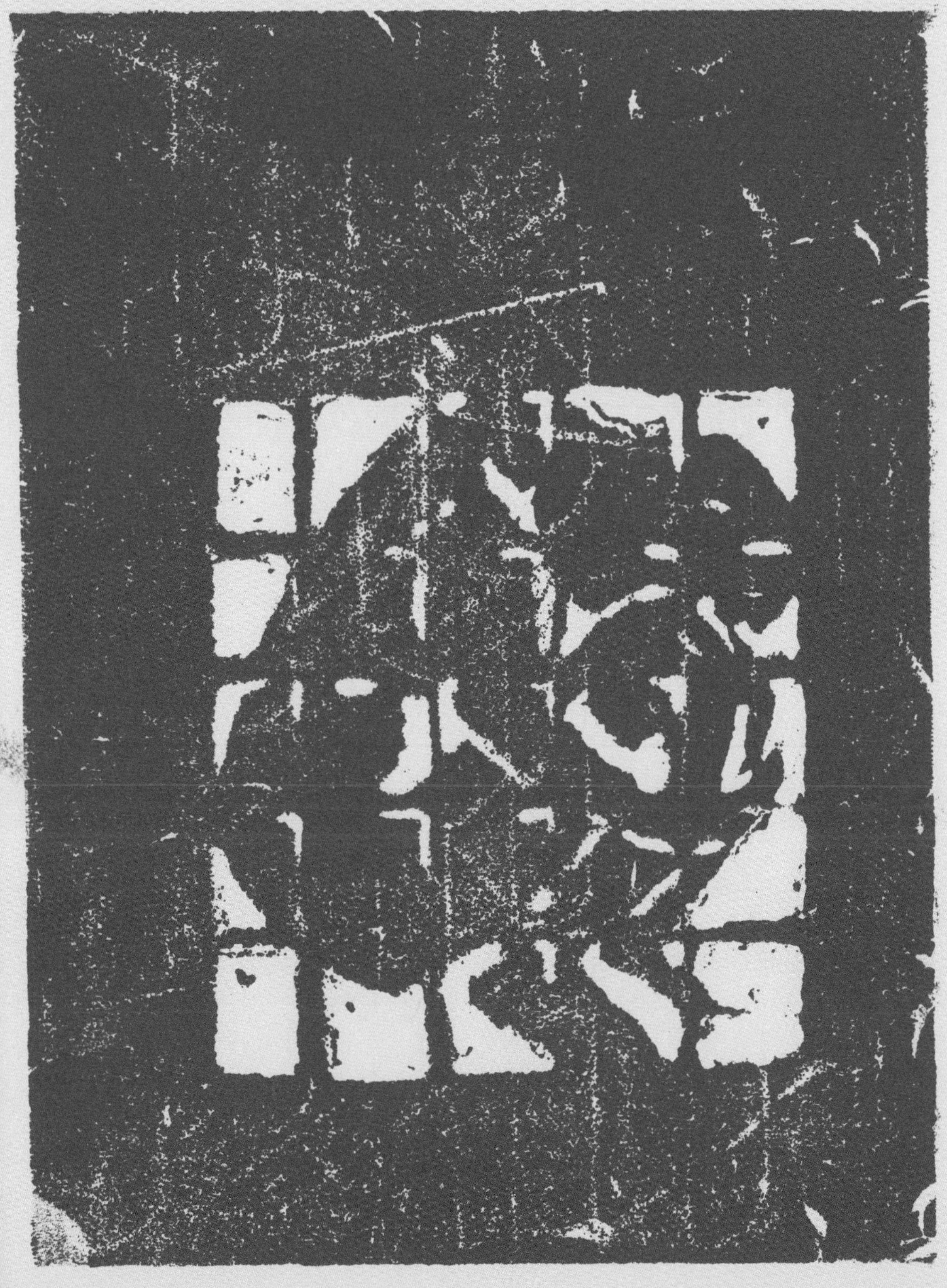

Darrell Wayne Fair, *Study*, 2016

Salvador Herrera, *UDHR Article 9* (Detail), 2018 »

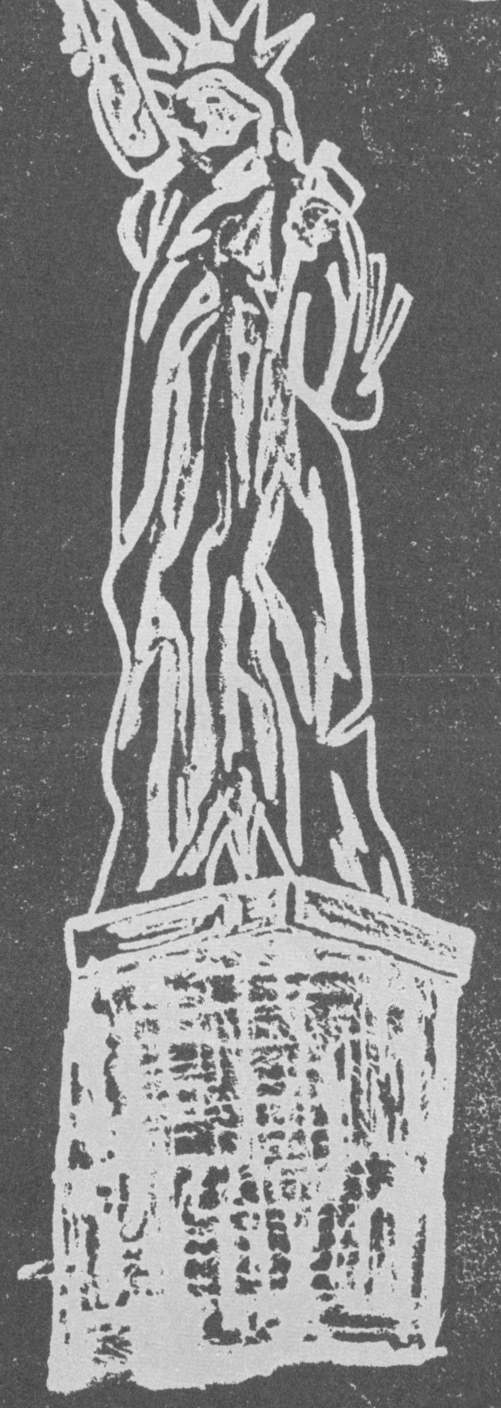
FREEDOM

To Be Human

To be human in America
means to be treated equal, right?!

To be human is not being
treated like 1/3 of a person.
I am a whole man not a piece
of one.

To be human. What does that
mean when you're treated like a
slave?!

To be human. How does that work
when you are locked in a jail cell
for 24 hours a day? Any sane person
will go crazy without no support to
keep them grounded mentally.

To be human is to be caring,
loving, supporting, respectful, and
overall teaching good morals.

To be human is taught from birth,
and must be practiced throughout
your whole life or you will become savage.

Pennies for the Opera

Our perfect confidence in the sun

In commemoration

every tambourine a thousand miles in every direction
                    playing in a California rent party

rattlers dancing and bleeding over God's non-whitened skin

waiting for the cornfield to shrug
            we are forgetful
            but your ancestors never the less

slowing down the poem to the speed of sweet light

the speed of bed-less deaths
the bones of fast friends near a pile of first fruits

                    a pile of imperialist failings

oppressor and oppressed give their guns the same nickname

underground working-class sort of goes back to school
                    sort of studies revolution

The summer belongs to itself now
As does a sharecropper's God
As does the death mask

Real advice from Malcolm
Real rose chords over my Memphis skeleton
            a tenor part before dying

playing to our waning blood pressure
our penny-plated gun (the last of the space-time) tucked

white people would have sold us standing naked on anything
sold us off a huge garden crystal
or peacock feather
would have sold us off of a stack of
doowop records if they could
would have sold us off of the
perfection of the cosmos

Forestry of drug paraphernalia
Suburb spikes in the grass
Syringe jungle like a sick bed's sick bed

execution needle that became a society's bottle neck
Preamble noose-talk
or nuclear scientist thanked for their work

Activists who don't scream Black power/rather Black component

A painful season
Season gone sentient
and well-dressed
taken as a whole
taken in puppet skin

a sentient Sunday that married fifteen sticks of dynamite

we are houseless now
and dancing our waistlines into a courtroom floor

Atlantic ocean throwing my voice into the city weeds
City weeds of the other other confederacy

I would double down on this poem
on this gang friendship

Tongo Eisen-Martin

signs of apocalypse in all directions
          I would run this poem into the ground

on my fifth skipped meal
          "today, Lord, we become even better friends"

dollar store notebooks in a mass context
pen cap full of bullets
California color line as played out with necro protest types who sleep on the other
other earth
While we are waiting to shoot on a muralist's behalf
                    This waiting to shoot: an old man's truancy of sorts
                    or tear stain on a Panther pamphlet

houseless bookseller speaking about little Bobby the conqueror

A crisis of open-air corrections
Chemical extradition
And war songs wearing off

                              Around the corner from South Texas
                              You pretended that prison is a river
                              You married your american cop

Black skin/white mantras

Like normal-speed bullets changing a normal life

Like walking back to the united states in defeat

JUS T

Sarah Ross

AFTERWORD

« Francisco Estrada, *Justice*, 2016

The struggle for human rights must begin with the struggle to be human. This simple fact might seem too obvious to acknowledge given the prevalence of rhetorical statements like "we all bleed the same blood" or "we're in this together." Yet settler colonialism and white supremacy are maintained through social practices—codes, laws, language and images—that suspend the humanness of many. As writers, artists and cultural producers, our role is to both reveal and undermine those practices as we build new imaginaries that refuse to compromise humanness, no matter the race, creed, gender, sexuality, ability, economic or geographical status of the human. For me, the following examples act as a north star. They map an art and discourse that both demands rights and also lays bare the often administrative forms of racist state violence.

In 1855, the state of Missouri tried and sentenced to death an enslaved woman for murder. Her name was Celia. Since the age of 14 she had been raped and abused by the white man who owned her, Robert Newsome, who she killed. In court, her claim of self-defense was denied based on the premise that she was enslaved, and therefore had "no self to defend." Celia's story framed a 2014 exhibition curated by Rachel Caidor and Mariame Kaba titled *No Selves To Defend*, featuring art and archival materials of criminalized survivors of violence. The exhibition served as a fundraiser for Marissa Alexander's defense, a Black woman sentenced to 20 years in prison for firing a warning shot after her husband attacked and threatened to kill her. Artists, including Billy Dee, Bianca Diaz, Molly Crabapple, and Micah Bazant, made portraits of Celia, Marissa, Joanne Little, Cece McDonald, Lena Baker, Inez Garcia, and other women who live in the dangerous intersection of being women of color who demand their right to live.[1]

More than a century after Celia's death sentence, Elmore Nickleberry, a sanitation worker and protester, participated in the 1968 Memphis sanitation

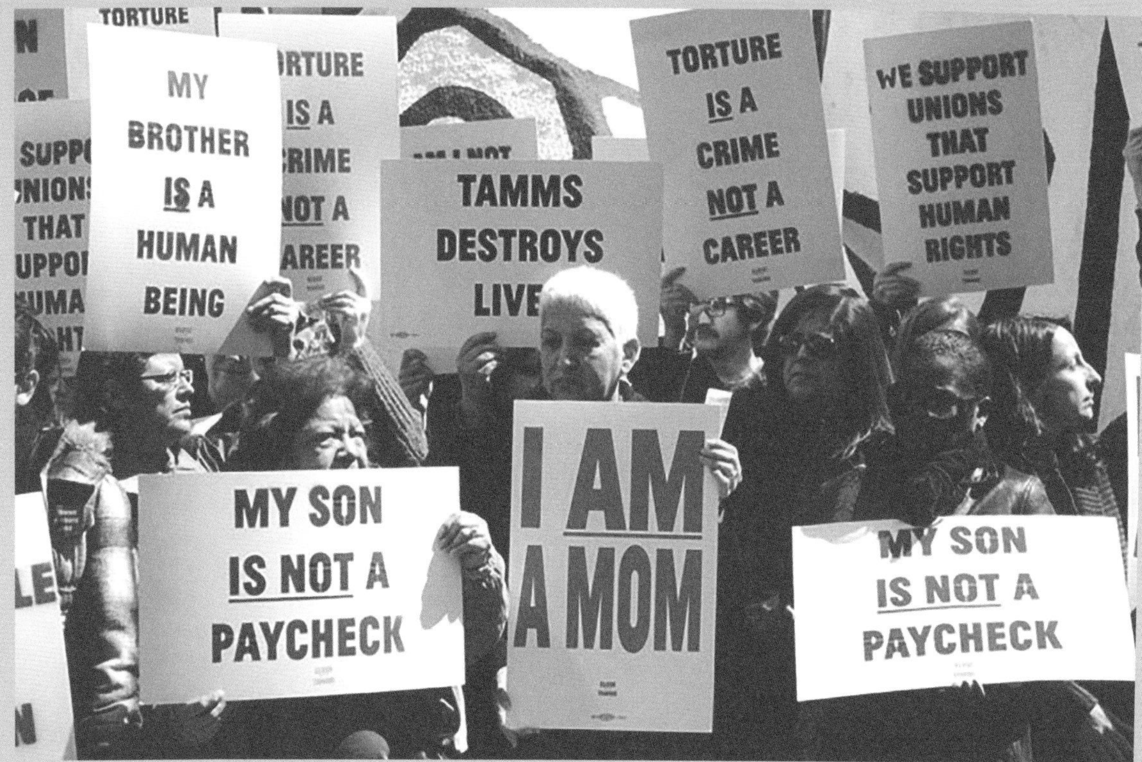

strike, which famously used the slogan "I Am a Man." Poignantly Nickleberry said, "*I knew I was a man… I just wanted a job to feed my family*" [emphasis mine].[2] The black and white posters held by sanitation workers stated something that was evident—the workers are men—yet in a nation with deep investments in white supremacy and settler colonialism, their rights as men (or humans) were systematically denied. As Nickleberry states the obvious of his humanness, it is not left there. Not only is he a man but he is a man with political and economic rights, articulated in the march itself.

The powerful words "I Am a Man" have been reprinted and remixed by artists and activists since the 1968 march. In 2012, they were used in a campaign for the rights of people in solitary confinement. Friends and family of incarcerated people in a group called Tamms Year Ten (named to highlight the 10 years that people languished in solitary confinement at Tamms supermax prison) marched to the headquarters of the AFSCME union that represented prison guards, with signs saying, "My Brother is a Man," "My Uncle is a Man" and "I Am A Mom."[3]

In the 1990s, artists and scholars made seminal works based on the

Photo by Adrianne Dues, April 4, 2012, courtesy Tamms Year Ten

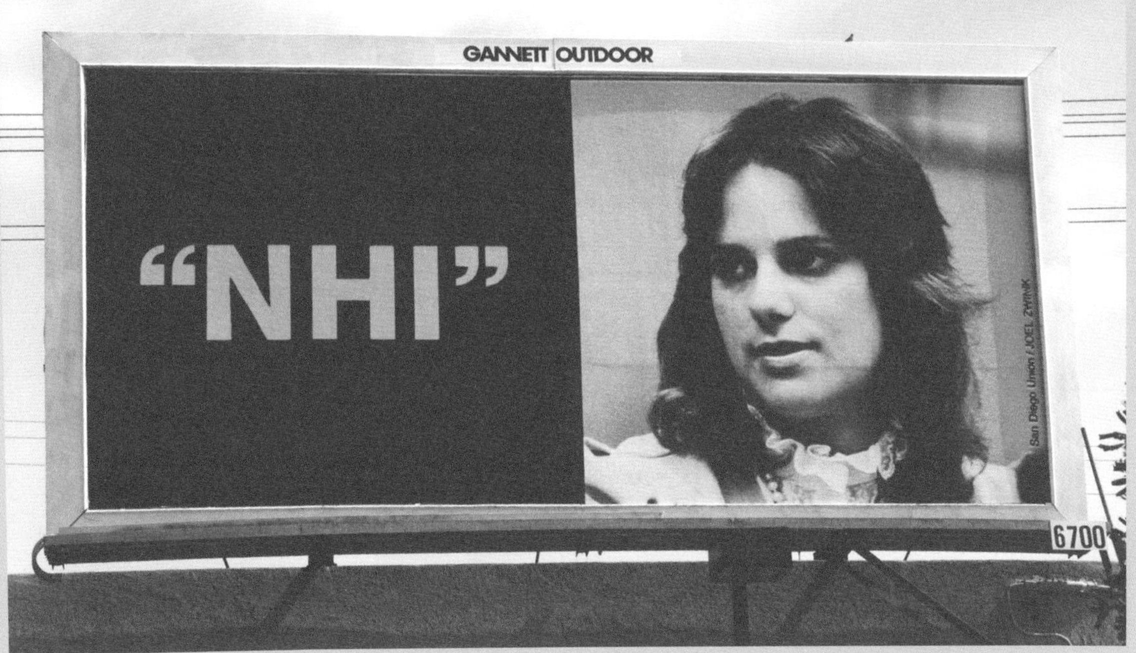

acronym NHI, a police term meaning "no humans involved" and used to refer to the deaths of marginalized people. Artists Deborah Small, Elizabeth Sisco, Scott Kessler, Carla Kirkwood, and Louis Hock created a series of public art projects, including two billboards featuring Donna Gentile with the letters NHI to bring attention to 45 women murdered in San Diego between 1985-1992. Gentile, a sex worker and police informant, was found brutally murdered after testifying against two police officers in San Diego. The deaths of other women were either caused by police involvement, or investigations of their deaths were mishandled or ignored by police. Portraits of all the women who were murdered were featured in a store front gallery that hosted discussions, events, and a performance of *Many Women Involved* by Kirkwood. While the term NHI was disputed by police at the time of the art projects, the *Sacramento Bee* newspaper quoted an officer saying, "These were misdemeanor murders, biker women and hookers ... we'd call them NHI's—no humans involved." A gallery book in the exhibition recorded an officer who wrote she "had been trained to disregard the humanity of victims from the darker side of life."[4] While the "darker side" surely was supposed to be a metaphor, it also reveals the wrenching truths of life lived in the long shadow of slavery and removal. Indeed, it is our darker sisters and brothers who are the targets of both state abandonment and state violence.

After the acquittal of police officers in the Rodney King beating in 1992, Sylvia Wynter wrote an influential essay titled "No Humans Involved: An Open Letter to My Colleagues." It again refers to and expands on the use of NHI by police "to any case involving a breach of the rights of young Black males who belong to the jobless category of the inner-city ghettos." Wynter suggests an "archipelago of Human Otherness" to describe the colonial present in which "Human Otherness can no longer be defined in terms of the interned Mad, the interned 'Indian,' the enslaved 'Negro' in which it had been earlier defined." Today, the archipelago is "... comprised of the jobless, the homeless, the poor, the systemically made jobless and criminalized."[5] For Wynter, human otherness is historically knitted in biocentric terms, meaning that the status of human is most certainly a racialized one. To articulate humanness is a constant praxis of counteracting that single metric of human—that of the white, middle class male.

I reflect on these artists and scholars as the heated summer of 2020 comes to a close and the murders of Breonna Taylor, George Floyd, Ahmad Aubrey, Dijon Kizzee, Miguel Vega, and the 780 other people killed by police this year (as of September) are still being protested in the streets. Artists, scholars, and poets return again and again to the prophetic words of Wynter, Franz Fanon, James Baldwin, and others as Black and Brown people are recast as dangerous, the violent ending of their short lives are justified as the outcome of their own making. In this context, which is not new, Christina Sharpe's book *In the Wake: On Blackness and Being* asks us to think about the possibilities of cultural work to "be a mode of inhabiting and rupturing this episteme with our known and lived un/imaginable lives." In beautiful and wrenching chapters Sharpe unravels poetry, film, and photos to examine the ways artists both reproduce and resist the violent spectacles of Black death and non-humanness. She says, "At stake is not recognizing antiblackness as total climate. At stake, too, is not recognizing an insistent Black visualsonic resistance to that imposition of non / being."[6]

With these examples—just a few of many—I want to tune us in to the "Black visualsonic resistance." What these images, words, and sounds tell us is that the struggle for human rights is first fought with the struggle to be human. That is to say, in the U.S., at all levels of the judicial system (a system that informs the behavior and policies of civil society), some of us are just not seen as human. In these examples, and throughout this book, we are confronted with the painful (and shameful) structures that render people non-human and also, the reverberations of resistance, beauty, and demands that say and enact: I have rights, I am human. The essays, poetry, and art shared here build on the history of Celia, Elmore Nickleberry, Carla Kirkwood and collaborators, Tamms Year Ten, Sylvia Wynter, Christina Sharpe, Mariame Kaba, Rachel Caidor, and others whose resistance emphatically embodies the ideal of human rights and also exposes the genocidal practices of the state who denies humanness. They show us that true, universal, and inalienable human rights are enacted often against the will of the state and they build a prefigurative formation that demands our freedom today and tomorrow.

---

1 Mariame Kaba, "No Selves to Defend: The Legacy of Criminalizing Self-Defense and Survival," No Selves to Defend, accessed September 19, 2020, https://noselves2defend.wordpress.com/.

2 "Stone Stories: Elmore Nickleberry," Stone Stories, Studio Gang, accessed September 20, 2020, https://studiogang.com/project/stone-stories.

3 Laurie Jo Reynolds and Stephen F. Eisenman, "Tamms is Torture: The Campaign to Close an Illinois Supermax Prison," Creative Time Reports, Creative Time, accessed September 10, 2020, https://creativetimereports.org/2013/05/06/tamms-is-torture-campaign-close-illinois-supermax-prison-solitary-confinement/.

4 Elizabeth Sisco, "Forum: Women Who Kill" in *Critical Condition: Women on the Edge of Violence*, ed. Amy Scholder (San Francisco: City Lights Books, 1993), 42-47.

5 Sylvia Wynter, "Unsettling the Coloniality of Being/Power/Truth/Freedom: Towards the Human, After Man, Its Overrepresentation—An Argument." *CR: The New Centennial Review* 3, no. 3 (2003): 257-337, doi:10.1353/ncr.2004.0015.

6 Christina Sharpe, *In the Wake: On Blackness and Being* (Durham: Duke University Press, 2016), 21-22.

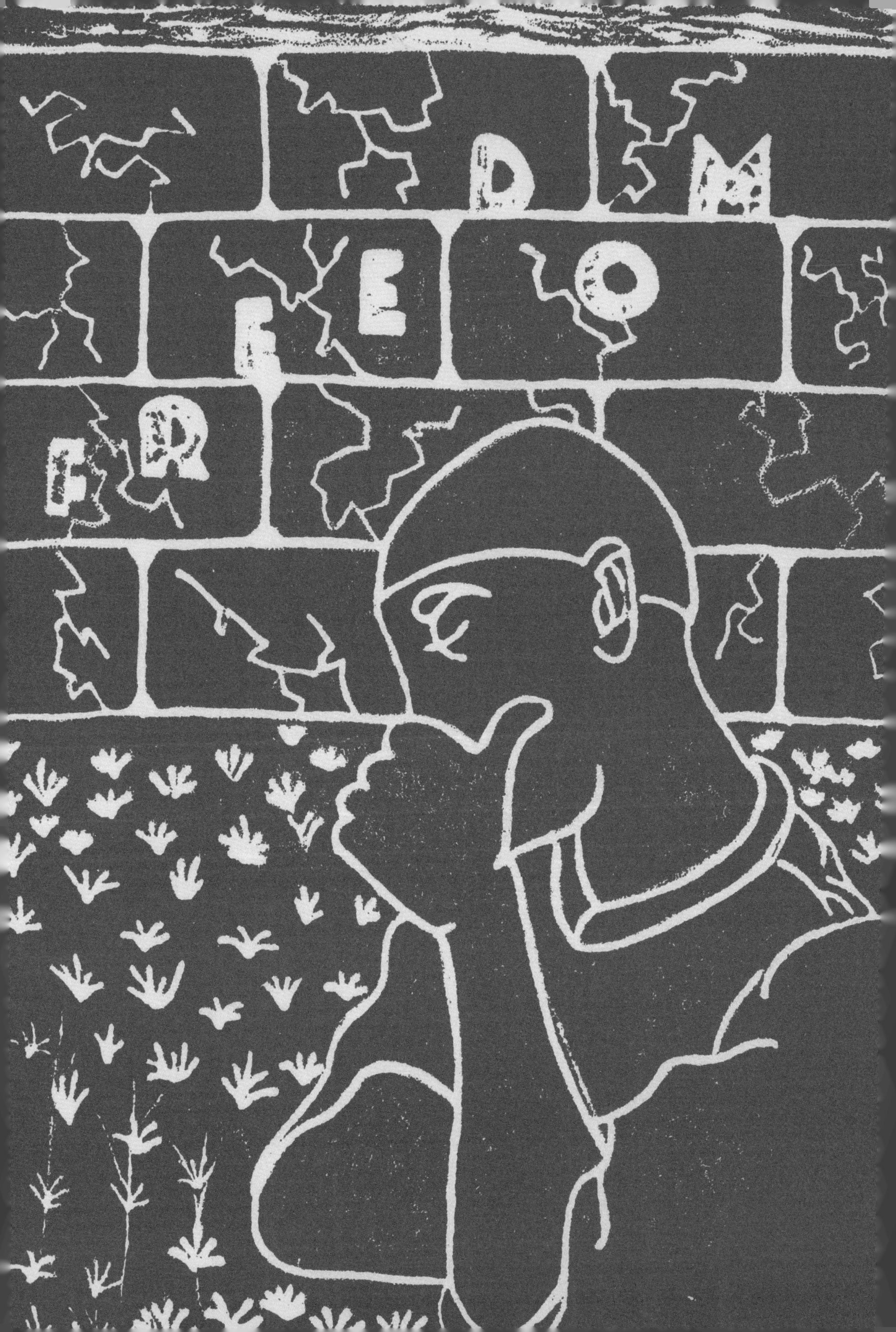

FREEDOM

Carlos Josúe Ayala is an American artist born in 1978 in Arecibo, Puerto Rico. He grew up on the northside of Chicago, where he graduated high school in 1997. After being incarcerated he gained the knowledge of different mediums to become a self-taught artist. While incarcerated Ayala has achieved his paralegal certificate and has become a painter, print-maker, and sketch artist. His art expresses a wide range of themes from race and violence to representing positive outlooks on life.

Tara Betts is the author of *Break the Habit, Arc & Hue*, and the forthcoming *Refuse to Disappear*. In addition to her work as a teaching artist and mentor for young poets, she has taught at several universities, including Rutgers University and University of Illinois-Chicago. Recently, she taught poetry workshops for three years at Stateville Prison. Betts is Poetry Editor at *The Langston Hughes Review* and the Lit Editor at *Newcity*.

Aryules Bivens was born in Chicago, Illinois on Oct. 5, 1962 and is now in his 37th year of wrongful imprisonment. During that time he earned an associate and bachelor degree and is working on a master's from North Park University. During his sentence he realized that an artist lives within him, thanks to P+NAP, who challenged him to go beyond his comfort zone of abstraction and cartoons. He has expanded the mediums he uses, which helps him cope and fight against this racist-oppressive criminal (wrong) justice establishment.

Eric Blackmon is a Chicago native and artist, poet, and paralegal at the MacArthur Justice Center. He spent more than 15 years in Illinois state prisons for a crime he didn't commit. He was represented by the Northwestern Center for Wrongful Convictions, which played an instrumental role in his release.

Blackmon works diligently to reform the system that once wrongfully incarcerated him. He is a member of the P+NAP and a student at Northeastern Illinois University.

Robert Boyd enjoys art because it does not constrict the thought process to small spaces, which allows for freedom at any given moment. He is a huge sports and football fan. He completed Barber College and is now in Northwestern's Prison Education Program as a third year student. He is working towards an associate's and then a bachelor's degree while pursuing his freedom.

Jeffery Campbell was raised in the Roseland Section on the South Side of Chicago. He is the father of three daughters, and a grandfather of two boys. He is in his second year of obtaining his associate degree in general studies from Northwestern University through Oakton Community College. He sees art and poetry as therapeutic and a beautiful way of expressing his deepest thoughts and feelings.

Alan "Wolf" Christensen is a divorced father of two and a grandfather of five kids. He was born and raised in the NW suburbs of Chicago. He does not have a formal education in art but appreciates all forms of art, especially music. He'd like to send a special thanks to Aaron Hughes in the P+NAP family.

Joseph Dole is currently serving a Life-Without-Parole sentence for a crime he did not commit. He is an award-winning and published writer, artist, and activist, has been incarcerated for over 22 years, and spent a decade in the notorious TAMMS supermax prison. He recently received his bachelor's degree from NEIU/UWW, focusing on Critical Carceral-Legal Studies. He is co-founder and policy director of Parole Illinois, an organization working for a more humane criminal-legal system. More of his work can be seen at facebook.com/JosephDoleIncarcerated.Writer. He can be contacted at JosephDole4paroleillinois@gmail.com or Joseph Dole K84446, Stateville C.C., PO Box 112, Joliet, IL 60434.

Tongo Eisen-Martin is a poet, movement worker, and educator originally from San Francisco. His latest curriculum on extrajudicial killing of Black People, We Charge Genocide Again, has been used as an educational and organizing tool throughout the country. His book *Someone's Dead Already* was nominated for a California Book Award. His latest book *Heaven Is All Goodbyes* was published by the City Lights Pocket Poets series, shortlisted for the Griffin Poetry Prize, and won a California Book Award and an American Book Award.

Martín Espada has published more than 20 books as a poet, editor, essayist, and translator. His forthcoming book of poems is called *Floaters* (2021). Other collections of poems include *Vivas to Those Who Have Failed* (2016), *The Trouble Ball* (2011), and *The Republic of Poetry* (2006). He is the editor of *What Saves Us: Poems of Empathy and Outrage in the Age of Trump* (2019). He has received the Ruth Lilly Poetry Prize, the Shelley Memorial Award, an Academy of American Poets Fellowship, and a Guggenheim Fellowship. Espada is a professor of English at the University of Massachusetts, Amherst.

Francisco Estrada was born and raised in Guadalajara, Jalisco, and came to Chicago when he was 11 years old. In prison he has learned all kinds of artistic mediums but prefers to work with acrylic. He loves to do all kinds of artwork from canvas to painting on clothing. He fights for his freedom so he can go to school and study art.

Darrell Wayne Fair was born Nov. 11, 1967 in Marvell, Arkansas. He is a contemporary American painter, animator and installation artist who explores race, criminal justice, and violence in his work. He is best known for his stylized self portrait that was exhibited at the Hyde Park Art Center in *The Weight of Rage* exhibition and also published on the cover of the April 2016 issue of *Poetry*. Fair is a graduate of Northeastern Illinois University.

torrin a. greathouse (she/they) is a trans poet, cripple-punk, and MFA candidate at the University of Minnesota. She has received fellowships from the Effing Foundation, Zoeglossia,

and the University of Arizona Poetry Center. Their work is published in *Ploughshares*, *New England Review*, *TriQuarterly*, and *The Kenyon Review*. She is the author of *Wound from the Mouth of a Wound* (Milkweed Editions, 2020).

Salvador Herrera was born and raised on the East Side of Chicago, Illinois. Art is his passion. It helps him express his feelings and also relaxes him. Art gives Herrera a chance to share his work with others, because art can mean a thousand words!

Renaldo Hudson survived a death sentence and a life without the possibility of parole sentence. He was finally granted clemency and released after 37 traumatic years of incarceration. Although he entered prison without the ability to read or write, Hudson was able to overcome this neglect obtaining multiple certifications, associate's degrees, and a seminary bachelor's degree while behind bars. He believes that our society needs to seek out the humanity of every person regardless of their charge or conviction. He is working with the Illinois Prison Project to end perpetual punishment.

Aaron Hughes is an artist, curator, organizer, teacher, antiwar activist, and Iraq War veteran. He works collaboratively in diverse spaces and media to create meaning out of personal and collective trauma, deconstruct and transform systems of oppression, and seek liberation. Working through an interdisciplinary practice rooted in drawing and printmaking, Hughes develops projects that deconstruct militarism and related institutions of dehumanization. These projects often utilize popular research strategies, experiment with forms of direct democracy, and operate in solidarity with the people most impacted by structural violence. Hughes works with projects including P+NAP, Justseeds Artists' Cooperative, About Face: Veterans Against the War, and emerging Veteran Art Movement.

Tyehimba Jess is the author of two books of poetry, *Leadbelly* and *Olio*. *Olio* won the 2017 Pulitzer Prize, the Anisfield-Wolf Book Award, The Midland Society Author's Award in Poetry, and received an Outstanding Contribution to Publishing Citation from the Black Caucus of the American Library Association. It was also nominated for the National Book Critics Circle Award, the PEN Jean Stein Book Award, and the Kingsley Tufts Poetry Award. *Leadbelly* was a winner of the 2004 National Poetry Series. Jess is a Professor of English at College of Staten Island.

Alice Kim is an educator, cultural organizer, and activist based in Chicago. She is Director of Human Rights Practice at The University of Chicago's Pozen Family Center for Human Rights. Alice teaches at a maximum-security prison in Illinois, leads the P+NAP's community building efforts across the prison wall, and is co-editor of *The Long Term: Resisting Life Sentence, Working Toward Freedom* (Haymarket Books, 2018). Alice is also a cofounder of Chicago Torture Justice Memorials, the group that initiated municipal reparations legislation for Chicago police torture survivors.

Alex Koehler is an artist and was a P+NAP scholar.

Juan Luna (born February 1974) is an artist/student who is currently incarcerated in Stateville CC. He's working on getting a bachelor's degree through the University Without Walls, Northeastern Illinois University. He is a strong believer in human rights. He plans to use his degree and art to bring people together in good times and in bad times. Luna also plans to become a well known artist in the future.

Timothy Malone was born and raised on the South Side of Chicago in the Englewood community. He aspires to become a motivational speaker to inform and encourage people to better themselves and each other. He is now a Christian who strives to love his neighbor as he loves himself.

Willie Moses McGee III is from Chicago's West Side Lawndale neighborhood. Most people call the part of town he lives in K-town. He loves art. It frees his mind and opens up his thought process. When people see McGee's art he wants them to see freedom of mind, body and soul.

Charles McLaurin was born and raised on the South Side of Chicago in Illinois. His evolution to becoming the artist he is today began at age 12, when his dearly beloved mother first introduced him to a dresser drawer stuffed with DC and Marvel Comics. McLaurin instantly became an avid reader who took the initiative to teach himself the creative process behind art by investing time and energy in the art section of any public library. His work made in P+NAP, including an animation titled "The Long Term," has been displayed at various venues around Chicago and the U.S.

Tony Medina is a poet, graphic novelist, editor, author, and the first Professor of Creative Writing at Howard University.

The author/editor of 21 books for adults and young people, including *Death, with Occasional Smiling*; *Thirteen Ways of Looking at a Black Boy*; *I Am Alfonso Jones*; and *Resisting Arrest: Poems to Stretch the Sky*, his poetry, fiction, and essays appear in over 100 anthologies and literary journals. Medina's books have garnered a number of awards, including the Paterson Prize for Books for Young People, the Langston Hughes Society Award, the first African Voices Literary Award, and both the Lee Bennett Hopkins Poetry Award honor and Special Recognition from the Arnold Adoff Poetry Award.

Zachary Meeks is a budding poet and fantasy novel writer. As an avid reader he sees poetry as a way to express one's emotions, much like other art forms such as dancing and singing. Originally from Ft. Payne Alabama, Meeks is the only child to a single mother. He was encouraged by his grandma to read instead of watching TV all day. From there his love of words and stories grew. Now his poetry and stories are the manifestation of that love.

Flynard N. Miller is an American-born artist from Chicago, Illinois. He is currently enrolled in the Northwestern Prison Education program, pursuing an Associate Degree in Liberal Arts. He's won numerous awards for his art. He also has earned an Associate of Theology. Miller's work can be seen on http://p-nap.org/longterm.html; http://paroleillinois. org/artwork; http://site.northwestern.edu/npep/ He can be contacted through: Connect Network.com.

Nikki Patin holds an MFA in Creative Nonfiction from the University of Southern Maine, is a recipient of a 3Arts Make A Wave award in music and was recently named one of "30 Writers to Watch" by the Guild Literary Complex. Patin is the Community Engagement Director for the Chicago Alliance Against Sexual Exploitation and the founder and Executive Producer of Surviving the Mic, a trauma-informed, survivor-led organization that hosts a weekly virtual brave space to support the writing and performances of survivors of sexual harm. Patín has taught, written and performed throughout the U.S., New Zealand, and Australia.

Rickey Lee Quezada, born August 6, 1983, is an artist and student housed at Stateville Correctional Center. Although he has been incarcerated as a juvenile, he has self-improved through education and programs he hopes to share with at-risk youth when he is released.

Barbara Ransby is a historian, writer, and longtime activist. She is a Distinguished Professor of African American Studies, Gender and Women's Studies, and History at the University of Illinois at Chicago (UIC) where she directs the campus-wide Social Justice Initiative. Prof. Ransby is author of the highly acclaimed biography, *Ella Baker and the Black Freedom Movement: A Radical Democratic Vision*; *Eslanda: The Large and Unconventional Life of Mrs. Paul Robeson* and *Making All Black Lives Matter: Reimagining Freedom in the 21st Century*.

Christophe Ringer is Assistant Professor of Theological Ethics and Society at Chicago Theological Seminary and author of *Necropolitics and the Religious Crisis of U.S. Mass Incarceration*. He received his Ph.D. in Religion, Ethics and Society from Vanderbilt University. His research interests include social ethics, public theology, political philosophy as well as the relationship of self, society, and the sacred in African American religion and culture. Ringer is an ordained minister and is active with a number of social justice organizations including A Just Harvest, Community Renewal Society, and Workers Center for Racial Justice. Ringer is married to Minister Kimberly Peeler-Ringer.

Benny Rios Donjuan grew up in the Pilsen community of Chicago and in the town of Cicero, Illinois. Currently he is a third year student earning a master's degree in Christian Ministry and Restorative Arts through North Park University and Theological Seminary. He aspires to be an agent of change in his quest to help heal our hurting communities from systemic racism and social ills. He has been incarcerated for over 18 years and longs to be united with his loving wife, his loving daughters, grandchildren, mom, brother, and loved ones.

Sarah Ross is an artist whose work addresses spatial concerns as they relate to access, class, anxiety, and activism. She co-founded the P+NAP and works with artists, activists, lawyers, torture survivors, and scholars on Chicago Torture Justice Memorials—a campaign for reparations for survivors of Chicago police torture. Her work has been exhibited in Los Angeles, New York, Montreal, Copenhagen, Rio De Janeiro, among other places. Ross is a Soros Justice Media Fellow and was awarded a Leaders for a New Chicago award from the MacArthur and Field Foundations. She is an Assistant Professor at the School of the Art Institute of Chicago.

Sonia Sanchez is an award-winning poet, activist, scholar, and formerly the Laura Carnell professor of English and women's studies at Temple University—is the author of 16 books, including *Like the Singing Coming off the Drums, Does Your House Have Lions?, Wounded in the House of a Friend,* and *Shake Loose My Skin*.

Meredith Stern works in printmaking, 'zine publishing, drumming, collage, gardening, and ceramic arts. She views art as a powerful medium of communication, which can call out injustice, visualize a more just world, and to celebrate the power of collective mutual aid and resistance. Since 2019 she has been on the board of directors of RIOTRI. She is a member of the Justseeds Artists' Cooperative and created the *Universal Declaration of Human Rights Print Project* this book is based on.

Marshall William Stewart has been housed at Stateville Correctional Center for a decade. During that time he has gained a paralegal diploma (2012), earned a bachelor's degree in Organizational Community and Resource Development for Non-Profits from Northeastern Illinois University (2019) and is currently completing his master's degree in Christian ministry with a Restorative Arts track (MACM-RA) from North Park University. Stewart is a Native American whose family resides on the Lac Du Flambeau Chippewa Reservation, and was raised by his Mexican American adoptive parents. He wants to be known for his love of his children and service for Jesus Christ.

Courtney Wright was born in Bronx, New York and moved to Chicago with his mother Yvette Wright at the tender age of two. Yvette migrated to Chicago to see a better life for her and her child. Unbeknownst to Yvette, America's racial social structure was designed to keep minorities in poverty. Wright believes through education our mentality and heart begins to change. Dr. Tara Betts educated Wright on art, poetry, culture and history. Wright has become a productive and positive man and a pillar of his community through education and self-help books. He is an emerging poet.

Salvador Herrera, *Pattern*, 2018

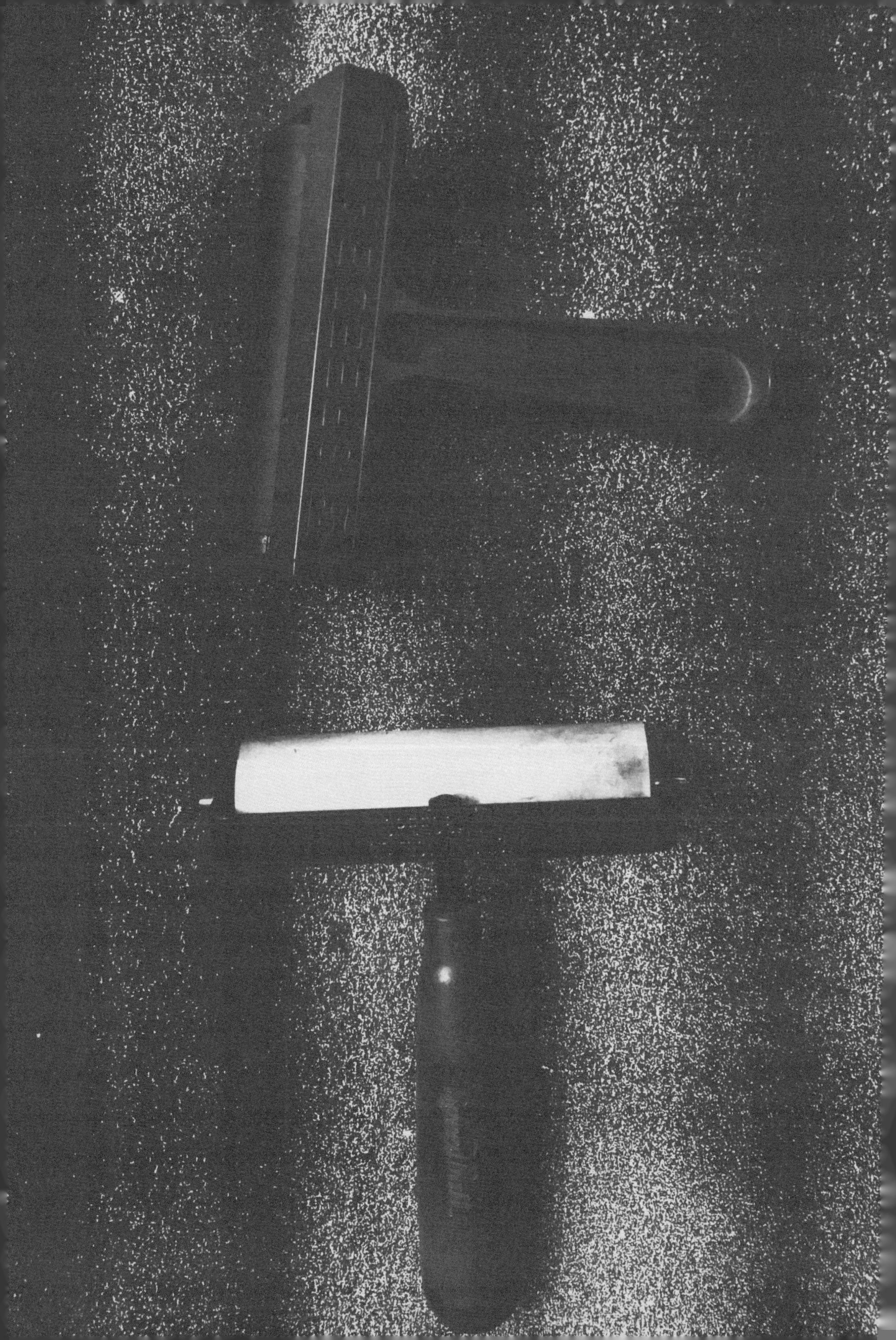